W9-CBF-752
3 3013 00058 1300

E
836
.A8
Albertson, Dean
Eisenhower as
president.
BRADNER LIBRARY
LIVONIA, MICHIGAN

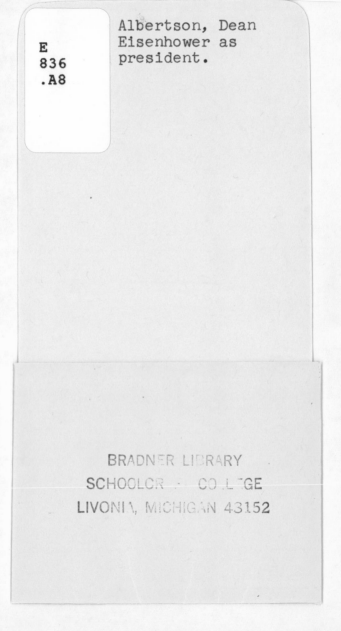

Eisenhower As President

Eisenhower As President

Edited and with an Introduction by

DEAN ALBERTSON

American Century Series

HILL AND WANG · NEW YORK

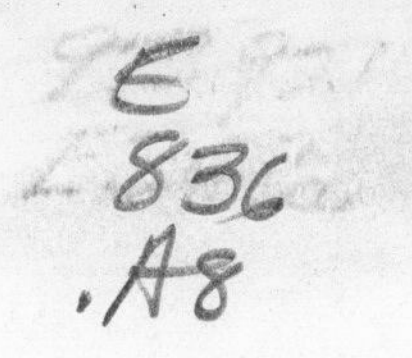

Library of Congress catalog card 63-8197

FIRST EDITION FEBRUARY 1963

Manufactured in the United States of America by
The Colonial Press Inc., Clinton, Massachusetts

To my mother, who, I suspect, liked Ike

CONTENTS

INTRODUCTION

THE DELEGATES to the 1952 Republican National Convention were forgathered hopefully to nominate the next American President. Presented with a choice between statesman Robert A. Taft of Ohio and army officer Dwight D. Eisenhower of the Normandy beachhead, the majority of them voted on the first ballot, not for the Senator whose public utterances were deemed by many to be the dogma of Republicanism, but for the General whose statements to that date had enunciated little more than patriotism and benevolence. The argument for expediency was conclusive; Eisenhower could win, Taft could not.

"We like Ike," the delegates chanted, and the candidate stepped forward in response to their approval. "I know something of the solemn responsibility of leading a crusade," he told them. "I have led one . . . Mindful of its burdens and of its decisive importance, I accept your summons. I will lead this crusade."

The aims of the crusade were set forth in gravity suitable to the occasion. Corruption was to be swept from the halls of government. The country was to receive a program of progressive policies drawn from the finest Republican traditions. Freedom was to be strengthened. A sound prosperity was to be built. A just and lasting peace throughout the world was to be sought.

No President of the United States ever entered office amidst more enthusiastic acclaim than did Eisenhower. No President has been more capable than he of evoking the warm respect and adulation of the American masses; nor was there the slightest evidence after he retired to Gettysburg or substantial diminution of his personal popularity. Nevertheless, within two years of his departure from Washington, there was ample evidence that informed reaction to Eisenhower's administrations was unfavorable. Ike still loomed an object of civic devotion while the conflicting aspirations of a perplexed electorate remained unresolved and unfulfilled. It was debated whether the crusade failed to measure accurately the tenor of the times, and to respond adequately and appropriately thereto, or whether the people accorded its mandate to a hero rather than to the leader of a political party whose announced policy he was expected to further. A third choice existed in the possibility that the American people knew exactly what they wanted, assayed the crusade correctly, and, having turned the electoral selector to the desired channel, sat back to watch the show.

"Good-by to the 'Fifties—and good riddance," Professor Eric Goldman wrote of the Age of Eisenhower. The era was one wherein, as Goldman viewed it, "we've grown unbelievably prosperous and we maunder along in a stupor of fat . . . We live in a heavy, humorless, sanctimonious, stultifying atmosphere, singularly lacking in the self-mockery that is self-criticism. Probably the climate of the late 'Fifties was the dullest and dreariest in all our history." [1]

New York *Post* editorialist William V. Shannon gauged civic response to the crusade at a similarly low level. "The Eisenhower years," he wrote, "have been years of flabbiness and self-satisfaction and gross materialism. . . . [The] loudest sound in the land has been the oink-and-grunt of private hoggishness. . . . It has been the age of the slob." [2]

Protestant clergyman Reinhold Niebuhr combined President and constituency in an analysis of America during the autumnal period of Eisenhower's tenure. "The President," observed Niebuhr, appeared to be "a decent but soft leader" symbolizing "both the essential decency and the love of ease of a great nation. If so," Niebuhr concluded, "the symbol may also indicate an anti-climax for the nation which speaks rather pretentiously and glibly of its 'moral leadership in the free world,' while living complacently in a hell of insecurity, consoled by its innumerable comforts, and failing to take the political measures requiring discipline and courage which would make that leadership effective." [3]

[1] Eric F. Goldman, "Good-By to the 'Fifties—and Good Riddance," *Harper's Magazine,* Vol. 220, No. 1316 (January 1960), p. 27.

[2] As quoted from Richard H. Rovere, "Eisenhower Over the Shoulder," *The American Scholar,* Vol. 31, No. 2 (Spring 1962), p. 176.

[3] Reinhold Niebuhr, "The Eisenhower Era," *The New Leader,* Vol. XLIII, No. 38 (October 3, 1960), pp. 3-4.

The Republican political campaign of 1952, insofar as it dealt with domestic issues, was not one to uplift or inspire adherents of the democratic faith. The opposition candidate, Governor Adlai E. Stevenson of Illinois, and his followers were derided as "intellectuals" and "eggheads," both terms of high opprobrium. Washington, so the press alleged, was rife with peculation of a degrading sort—mink coats and deepfreezes were mentioned frequently as part of the Democratic boodle. The economy, businessmen were assured, had too long rested in unsafe hands—"soundness" should be restored. And then there were, of course, the hordes of Communists who, according to the meretricious imagination of Senator Joseph McCarthy, had infested the State Department for Moscow's purposes.

Abroad, the problems were more real than imagined. The aggressive expansion of the Soviet Union at the conclusion of World War II had carried a virulent form of totalitarianism across Eastern Europe, through the Balkans and beyond Berlin, leaving a city free among the unfree and an international sore which was bound to fester repeatedly. The brilliant logistical campaign of the Berlin airlift had saved the city temporarily, and a Cold War military "containment" offensive had been mounted by President Harry Truman under the North Atlantic Treaty Organization alliance. Marshall Plan aid, the second major aspect of Democratic foreign policy, was provided to restore the economic health of Western Europe. Finally, a Point Four program of technical assistance sought to remove poverty and weakness in underdeveloped areas as elements most susceptible to Soviet suasion.

In the Far East, America had been committed by the Truman administration to full support of the United Nations in throwing the North Koreans back across the 38th parallel. It was a conflict to which the American people were presumed to have acquiesced, but it became, particularly after the disastrous retreat from the Yalu River, an immensely unpopular enterprise marked by little discernible advance and ever lengthening casualty lists. Worse, it was a war for which no possible victory could be envisaged save at peril of direct engagement with the Russians and Chinese themselves. Considering the rapid advance of Soviet thermonuclear arms and the corresponding snail-like development of Russian international political responsibility, few were willing to entertain the possibility of action against Soviet military might. The massive population of China had been, by Republican interpretation, "lost" to the enemy, with the exception of Chiang Kai-shek's meager force "leashed" on the offshore islands of which Taiwan was the largest. Completing the catalogue of catastrophe to American interests, the leaders and masses of South Asia, the Middle East, and Latin America remained for the most part incomprehensively aloof from commitment to the side of truth and justice.

Such indeed were problems to invite the attention, if not introspection, of United States citizens and leaders alike. Yet it may be doubted that Dwight D. Eisenhower carried with him to the White House a mandate to do more than to end the Korean stalemate, to expunge the revealed venialities of the Truman administration, and to maintain "the American Way of Life."

The style of the early fifties, unlike the style of the mid-thirties, was stamped heavily with private concern, not public necessity. Crusades of all descriptions were publicly well received and privately set aside in the rush of business of those who had more important matters afoot. The stirring battles for social justice of the New Deal period, assumed to have been won and embedded in appropriate legislation, were now safely tucked away in history beside the small clothes of Jefferson and the artillery pieces of the Potomac army. Tales of glory repetitiously related by slightly balding veterans of World War II were regarded with condescension by younger listeners—nor was a sizable number of the veterans themselves on hand to re-enlist in another similar venture without duress. Time spent in Iwo's volcanic ash or amid the hedgerows of Brittany had been time lost in the race for profits and status. Had Calvin Coolidge arisen to repeat in the fifties his famous aphorism of the twenties, "the business of America is business," he would have been close to the mark. Despite the size of the convention vote for "internationalist" Ike in preference to "isolationist" Taft, it was a minority of the electorate who understood that isolationism was no longer relevant to the American situation, that German V-2 rockets presaged a time when oceans would be as rivulets in relation to national military security, that the atomic age had ushered in an era in which total war could mean total human destruction and total victory was made a dream of the past, and that the platitudes of domestic politics could neither exorcise enemies abroad nor correct injustice within the national household.

The crusade campaign, reassuring the public that American boys soon would be home from Korea, stern in moral abjuration of the "mess in Washington," muted in response to McCarthy demagoguery, and imprecise about overthrowing the Democratic welfare program, presented its case to the people. Americans seemed approving of that which Ike said the Republicans would do for them, and selectively inattentive to whatever demands on their time the crusade hesitantly made. In any case, none could deny the efficacy of the approach when the votes were counted.

Before taking office, Eisenhower made his much-publicized trip to Korea and soon after inauguration the Republicans redeemed their campaign promise to end the hated conflict. It was of little consequence to the American people whether the armistice signed at Panmunjom came about because of administration "peace or else" policy, as part of the thrust-and-withdraw tactics of Soviet diplomacy, or as a result of Stalin's death. Further bloodshed in that bleak land was unsupportable. American soldiers would, for a time, cease to perish in the ill-understood cause of mutual security. The extraordinary popularity of the new President was easily comprehended by all but the most obtuse. Having gained its first point, the Administration then turned to correct the maladministration of its predecessor in Washington.

In the minds of the President's advisors, the executive establishment had lost dignity during the past two decades because, so they said, it had become an operating branch of government. Labor disputes, aeronautics and trade decisions, administrative and operational details of all varieties, as well as the dispensation of patronage, all came to the White House for adjudication. Eisenhower believed that the President should divest himself of such pressures. His White House was to be the place from which National Policy alone would emerge. The detail work of carrying out the policy was to be relegated to less lofty levels of government. Between the President and his Cabinet it was agreed that decentralization and delegation of authority were to be the order of the day. "You have full authority. I expect you to stand on your own feet," Eisenhower is said to have told them. "Whatever you decide goes. The White House will stay out of your hair." [4] As Merlo Pusey, Washington *Post* editorial writer and admiring Eisenhower biographer saw it, "a sweeping evolution" had taken place. No longer was the chief executive "a lone figure in an ivory tower, but the director of a great organization. Eisenhower completed the transformation of the office into an institution. His ability to function as the captain of a team and to gather around him an official family with enough responsibility and *esprit de*

[4] Charles J. V. Murphy, "Eisenhower's White House," *Fortune,* Vol. 48 (July 1953), p. 75.

corps to carry on in his absence has given the Presidency new strength and stability in time of emergency." [5]

Sherman Adams, an Assistant to the President and spokesman for the new management, defined his own role as being "neither to functionalize or institutionalize, but rather to departmentalize" [6] —terminology presumably understood by his listeners. It was Adams's task each morning to assemble and direct the staff in its assignment as a "clearinghouse" on policy, and to assist the staff in screening out matters of minor importance which would only clog the Presidential calendar. In addition, he directed the compressing of policy summations in accordance with the debatable Eisenhower maxim, "If a proposition can't be stated in one page, it isn't worth saying." With Press Secretary James Hagerty, Adams also shared the duty of making critical judgments regarding which White House visitors might be admitted to see the President. While the new managerial techniques assuredly absolved General Eisenhower from all taint of authoritarianism often attributed to the military and seemed to place him in thought alongside the philosophers of industry, it had certain drawbacks. It divorced policy from function with certain appalling results, such as in the case of the U-2. It strained relations with Senators and Congressmen whose political fortunes were partially measured in terms of intimacy with the President. Finally, the staff screening approach left the Chief of State shielded from dissenting comment and advice. However, it lightened the work load and allowed the President some time to pursue his private mode of life.

There is little reason to suppose the citizenry as a whole disapproved Eisenhower's recreational habits. His reading consisted largely of western paperback novels. As he revealed at a press conference, his perusal of newspapers was desultory at best: "I take the, what I call the more important sections of the Sunday papers that review world events, go over the things, and those are the things I study carefully. The things you talk of, cartoons and unfriendly quips, I just can't be bothered." [7] His paintings, held in high esteem as mementos, were not intended to compete in professional circles. His occasional bridge games and frequent resort to the golf links (according to *U. S. News and World Report,* over six hours on the day federal troops arrived at Central High School in Little Rock, Arkansas) were standard recreation for

[5] Merlo J. Pusey, *Eisenhower the President* (New York, Macmillan, 1956), pp. 285-286.

[6] Murphy, "Eisenhower's White House," p. 76.

[7] *Newsweek,* Vol. 55, No. 21 (May 23, 1960), p. 72.

large parts of the American middle class. While no one was apt to confuse Eisenhower with the "eggheads," neither could the critic overlook his apparent humanitarianism, his genuine decency, and above all the high sense of moral purpose which underlay his undoubted concern for the welfare of the nation.

Eisenhower's economic philosophy, Presidential Aide Gabriel Hauge told the membership of San Francisco's Commonwealth Club, "recognizes the primacy of moral values in a material world." Hauge, who played a substantial part in bringing forth the philosophy, called his address the "Economics of Eisenhower Dynamic Conservatism." [8] The body of the doctrine made sense, however, particularly to Americans who cast longing eyes back into the twenties. To Eisenhower "business—whether little, medium-sized or big—is a good word, because business is people." "Business," Hauge continued with an air of rhetorical innovation, "is one of the most pervasive manifestations of America. It is the way a whole people organizes its economic life. The Eisenhower conservative deplores its reckless denunciation, either directly, as when its moral basis is attacked, or indirectly, as when attempts are made to drive out or keep out of government service those who have risen in its ranks." This aspect of Dynamic Conservatism at least twice occasioned inquiry among the Cabinet regarding possible conflict of interest. The remainder of the philosophy delicately updated rugged individualism to conform to the obvious demands of the fifties. The President, "not much taken" with notions of federal price fixing and wage control "except, of course, in time of war," wanted to conserve free markets and private initiative. His was a "deep conviction that in the economic race every man should have an equal place at the starting line. . . ." He was "cognizant of the thievery and worse that price inflation visits on the citizenry. . . ." Nevertheless, the Eisenhower conservative sought "to conserve the market mechanism when the government must act to avert a depression or inflation." [9]

There was little here with which free enterprise might quarrel unless one wished to take issue with the evasions used to disguise the "moderative" character of the Eisenhower government. The words, meant to rally the conservative Republican faithful to the crusade, belied an internal policy which maintained and occasion-

[8] Gabriel Hauge, "Economics of Eisenhower Dynamic Conservatism," a reprint of an address made before the Commonwealth Club of San Francisco, California, October 14, 1955, in *The Commercial and Financial Chronicle,* Vol. 182, No. 5476 (October 27, 1955), pp. 1, 28-29.

[9] *Ibid.*

ally improved upon the welfare aims of the New Deal. For all its semantic incongruity, Dynamic Conservatism was apparently what the people wanted—a program which would march forth in sound and fury signifying no real change in the tenets of Rooseveltian capitalism. However mightily Eisenhower strove to balance the budget, it would remain unbalanced. The assiduous attempts of Treasury Secretary Humphrey to pursue a tightened credit policy led only to threatened recession and back to loosened credit. The American economy was, by consensus, less subject to the moral values presumably inherent in Dynamic Conservatism than it was to popular demand for domestic acquisition of goods and continuance of the foreign dialogue.

Morality was also a fixture of Eisenhower's foreign policy. In this realm, however, the precepts of goodness announced as cornerstones of diplomacy brought principally an unending torrent of abuse from the right, the left, and from allies overseas.

McCarthy-sympathizer William F. Buckley, Jr., writing for *The National Review,* was disturbed at the "perverse . . . stubborn . . . invincible ignorance" of a President who could not comprehend that the Soviet atomic arsenal existed to be dropped on people. "Rather than lift that last veil and behold the shocking designs of human beings against other human beings, he [Eisenhower] slips back into his familiar world of copybook homilies; back to the world he learned about at his mother's knee." [10]

Former Secretary of State Dean Acheson aired his views on Presidential moralism in *The Reporter* magazine shortly after the Suez affair. Eisenhower, he said, had "found a satisfyingly firm stance in what he has continually referred to as 'moral and spiritual values.' These values are not more specifically defined than 'Honesty, decency, fairness, service'—all that sort of thing. . . . Since the values he stresses are moral and spiritual values, the power he refers to is moral power. The only source of moral power is moral rightness, and moral power is the dominant power. Pascal, who was not a cynic . . . said: 'Justice without power is impotent; power without justice is tyranny.' " Acheson concluded with a warning against moralistic legalism: "It induces a state of mind which leads our government to say—and even worse, perhaps to think—that the United States has no ambitions and desires in the Middle East. We do have desires. We do have interests—vitally important ones. And the idea that we are engaged on a crusade or

[10] William F. Buckley, Jr., "The Tranquil World of Dwight D. Eisenhower," *The National Review,* Vol. 5, No. 3 (January 18, 1958), p. 58.

mission to vindicate a vaguely and erroneously conceived 'moral law' has led to actions which, I fear, are quite contrary to our interests." [11]

Hans J. Morgenthau, Director of the University of Chicago Center for Study of American Foreign Policy, deplored the evaporation of American diplomacy "into an amorphous fog of irrelevant platitudes" which left the nation with only "two extreme choices, both incompatible with the national interest: retreat and violence, neither subject to rational limitations." Professor Morgenthau was disheartened when he surveyed Republican policy. "When we heard spokesmen for the government propound the legal and moral platitudes which had passed for foreign policy in the interwar period, we thought that this was the way in which the government . . . tried to make the stark facts of foreign policy palatable to the people. They were—so it seemed to us—the tinsel in the show window making the merchandise on the counter attractive to the customer. We were mistaken. Those platitudes *are* the foreign policy of the United States. The counter is bare; that tinsel is all the store has to sell. Hence the alarm, the sadness, and the sorrow." [12]

If consensus had been reached by the American people on the proposition that the economic and social changes wrought by the New Deal were not to be withdrawn, only placed under new management, it might likewise be argued that a similar consensus had been agreed to in the realm of foreign policy. America, so Franklin D. Roosevelt and Harry Truman patiently led their countrymen to understand, was part of the world. Roosevelt's ultimate foreign policy was designed specifically to stamp out the evil which was Nazism, to defeat the Japanese who had attacked America in the Pacific, and to involve the United States in the United Nations. Truman, realistically aware of America's inability to exterminate Communism abroad, sought to combat Russian expansion by means of U.N. tribunals and to contain Soviet influence within boundaries least harmful to the United States and her allies.

President Eisenhower and his Secretary of State, John Foster Dulles, needed to give a "New Look" to American diplomacy while maintaining congressional bipartisanship. The two men, sharing a well-intentioned belief in America's moral rightness, were faced by two bellicose and often overlapping contingents within the

[11] Dean Acheson, "Foreign Policy and Presidential Moralism," *The Reporter,* Vol. 16, No. 9 (May 2, 1957), pp. 12-14.

[12] Hans J. Morgenthau, "The Decline and Fall of American Foreign Policy," *New Republic,* Vol. 135, No. 24 (December 10, 1956), p. 12.

nation. One desired to "unleash" the small Chinese Nationalist force on Taiwan to reclaim the Asian mainland. The other, comprising by Gallup Poll estimate 50 percent of the American people, believed Senator McCarthy's irresponsible outbursts about internal subversion were doing as much good as harm. However misguided, public opinion demanded that something be done about Communists at home and abroad. The result was an aggressively anti-Communist policy, abounding in moral rectitude, but faced off by the countervailing atomic power of Soviet arms. What Dulles and the President seemed to be contemplating was the liberation of Russian satellite peoples. As it became obvious that Americans had something much less risky in mind than armed liberation, the lexicon of the New Look ("massive retaliation"—"brinkmanship"—"bigger bang for the buck"—"agonizing reappraisal") became horrifying to lovers of peace and searchers after rational foreign policy. The dream that America's right could alone make might was blasted finally at Suez and in Budapest. America's friends, Britain and France, angrily withdrew from Egypt, and a few thousand Hungarians fortunate enough to escape the consequences of their imprudence were given sanctuary in the United States.

Hans Morgenthau agreed that Eisenhower had not been elected on the strength of his platform, but rather as a symbol of the nation's longing for peace, an image which Morgenthau saw as reflecting Ike's own conception of the Presidency in theory and practice. "Supported by an optimistic philosophy, unaware of man's propensities for evil and the tragic dilemmas of human existence, he has limited himself, by and large, to the enunciation of general principles, leaving the political task of their implementation to subordinates or to nobody in particular. . . ." Thus, Morgenthau concluded, "the President, by divorcing his person and his office from the partisanship of politics, has transformed the character of politics itself. . . . Everybody seems to emulate the President's example and rise above politics, sharing in the nobility of his sentiments and general objectives. The result is national unity, paid for with the life-blood of the democratic process. For this is not the unity of a people who, after weighing the alternatives, have decided what they want. It is rather like a fog that makes us all brothers in blindness." [13]

Was the public awed by the complexity of national problems in the age of the expert, or did they abdicate their democratic choice

[13] Hans J. Morgenthau, "What the President and Mr. Dulles Don't Know," *New Republic,* Vol. 135, No. 25 (December 17, 1956), pp. 14-15.

in favor of those who provided tranquillity through moderation? Harvard history professor Oscar Handlin said it was the failure of leadership, both congressional and executive, to define the issues. "In the cheerfully vague oratory of the time," said Handlin, "peace is a way to liberate the satellites, strategic retreats in every part of the globe strengthen a military position, and small, cheap armies, under God, are more powerful than large, expensive ones—and better for the budget. Moderation is thus good, and good for you. In the context of this past, moderation means evading the necessity of choice, the suspense of inaction between undesirable alternatives. After twenty years of confused striving, the voters value above all else the appearance of peace and stability that the Eisenhower administration has given them." [14]

Newspaper feature writer Sidney Hyman, author of *The American President,* noted that the dominating tendencies of the Eisenhower Presidency "have been to act as if domestic and foreign affairs were separate matters; as if religion was a substitute for politics in a condition of no war and no peace; as if a balanced budget was the paramount means of meeting the Soviet economic offensive; as if he could win the newly emergent nations to the practice of democracy by ringing democratic manifestoes—while withholding from them a full measure of the material assistance they need as flooring for democratic growth." [15] But, above all, Eisenhower had failed, according to Hyman, to understand a significant twentieth-century change in the Presidency which prescribed that the Executive was expected to lead from above while Congress revised and vetoed from below.

William V. Shannon called Eisenhower a transitional figure. "He has not shaped the future nor tried to repeal the past. He has not politically organized nor intellectually defined a new consensus. When he leaves office . . . the foreign policies and the domestic policies of the past generation will be about where he found them in 1953. No national problem, whether it be education, housing, urban revitalization, agriculture, or inflation, will have been advanced importantly toward solution nor its dimensions significantly altered. The Eisenhower era is the time of the great postponement." [16]

[14] Oscar Handlin, "Do the Voters Want Moderation? The Politics of Evasion," *Commentary,* Vol. 22, No. 3 (September 1956), p. 198.

[15] Sidney Hyman, "The Failure of the Eisenhower Presidency," *The Progressive,* Vol. 24, No. 5 (May 1960), p. 12.

[16] William V. Shannon, "Eisenhower as President: A Critical Appraisal of the Record," *Commentary,* Vol. 26, No. 5 (November 1958), p. 390.

Richard Rovere, columnist for the *New Yorker* and author of *Affairs of State: The Eisenhower Years,* saw little to regret in Eisenhower's first term of office. Tensions were eased. The Korean war was terminated. Corruption and McCarthyism were extirpated. Nevertheless, he added, "If there was anything much to be said [for the second four years], it has escaped my notice and understanding. By 1956, the tasks that had seemed to call for the bland Eisenhower treatment had all received it, and the rest, in Washington anyway, was drift and near-slumber." [17]

Merlo Pusey, in his book *Eisenhower the President,* also saw "substantial progress" during the first Eisenhower Administration in arresting the spread of Communism, strengthening free world ties, revitalizing the free enterprise system, and infusing "a new dynamism into our mature democratic society." In the closing lines of his volume Pusey asked: "Can the man from Abilene be numbered, then, among our great Presidents?" Pusey's answer: "Some of his qualities are admittedly ordinary. Despite his ability to move people, he is not a great orator and writer as is Churchill. He is not a great innovator or philosopher. His domestic reforms are not outstanding beside those of his immediate predecessors. His period in the White House has not been as dramatic as were the Presidential years of Washington, Lincoln, Wilson, and Franklin D. Roosevelt. . . . President Eisenhower will occupy a great and distinctive place of his own in our national folklore. And it is by no means improbable that his standing will be as high in the political world as it already is in our military history." [18]

Pusey's summation of the President's capabilities, written in 1956, was but a forerunner of estimates to come. Whether the presumed fault in Eisenhower's approach to statecraft lay in moderation, postponement, drift, or misinterpretation of changing function, the preponderance of journalistic and historical opinion was, by the early 1960's, certain that the man from Abilene would not be numbered among America's great Presidents.

At the same time, it might be argued that the democratic mechanism still functioned to cast upon the national scene precisely the type of Chief Executive reflecting the *set* and *style* of the American people themselves. And it would be difficult to ascribe to the mass of Americans qualities of reflection, aspiration, or perception markedly different from those of Eisenhower.

[17] Richard Rovere, "Eisenhower Over the Shoulder," *American Scholar,* Vol. 31, No. 2 (Spring 1962), p. 178.

[18] Pusey, *op. cit.,* pp. 294-295.

The United States at the end of World War II was, for the average American, open, on the one hand, to provide unparalleled prosperity for the nation with the highest living standard on earth. On the other hand, it was for Americans a world bounded by the rejected dogma of Karl Marx, the gloomy predictions of Thomas Malthus, the hauntingly unanswered questions of Sigmund Freud, and the disturbing formulae of Albert Einstein. As the simple certainties of virtue's rewards had come to be replaced for the new Organization Man by status judgments, the frontier doctrine of individualism lost relevance for the masses in the creation of bigger labor organizations, bigger corporations, and bigger bombs.

In the resultant confusion, the American people, alternately piqued and threatened by the Russians between 1953 and 1961, confronted with a new situation defined neither as peace nor war, bedeviled by massive problems of urban living, and entranced with the debatable luxury of credit-card prosperity, responded to the stimuli of their times with full garbage pails on weekdays and a return to God on the Sabbath. As automotive tailfins grew higher, church and temple attendance increased. While installment buying fed indulgence in the economic sector, debate ranged in the private sector over battery additives, polio vaccine, fluoridation, bomb shelters, atomic testing, school subsidization, and Jim-Crowism. Television ratings of horse operas and situation comedies rose, and so did the public purchase of quality paperback literature and serious musical recordings.

If, as William V. Shannon suggested, Americans of the fifties were "slobs" living, as Reinhold Niebuhr observed, in a hell of insecurity consoled by innumerable comforts, no firm voice from Armageddon exhorted these same Americans to high purpose, nor did Americans appear eager to respond to such a summons. The clangor of cash registers and the screed of marching peace pickets were sounds of the fifties almost loud enough to drown the arching roar of Sputnik I. It was against this multicolored backdrop that Dwight D. Eisenhower evoked the crusade. And these were the Americans whom he was elected to lead. They liked Ike.

Dean Albertson

Brooklyn College
November 1962

SHERMAN ADAMS

At Work in the White House

EISENHOWER always wanted his weekly meetings with the Cabinet, the National Security Council, and the legislative leaders, and, on other days, his most important business appointments, to be scheduled for the earliest possible hour of the morning, eight o'clock if at breakfast, eight-thirty, or nine o'clock at the office. This required some members of his official family to make a drastic change in their habits of living. Noting one day that Herbert Brownell had some difficulty in getting to an early Cabinet meeting on time, Eisenhower jocularly held up his Attorney General as an example of "one of those big city boys who need their sleep in the morning." One reason why I worked well with Eisenhower was that I shared his eagerness to be on the job early. I found that among people in high places in Washington this was regarded as odd behavior but it was a habit that I could not break because I had been doing it all of my life. I found it a useful habit because Eisenhower's staff was no place for anybody who had trouble getting to work at seven-thirty.

At that hour I usually met with Tom Stephens to go over some items on the President's work schedule for the day. A check with Ann Whitman, the President's personal secretary, another early riser, often revealed the Eisenhower mood, which was of great help in smoothing out the arrangements for the day's activities. Mrs. Whitman could catch the scent of trouble when the rest of the staff was oblivious to an impending crisis. "The President isn't very happy with the remarks for the Chamber of Commerce meeting this morning," she would confide. That was a signal for me to find out why the President wasn't happy with the remarks and to see to it that something more solid was provided.

If it was a Wednesday, the day that Eisenhower had his weekly press conference, I called the key members of the staff together for breakfast with Jim Hagerty in the basement mess hall of the White House that was operated by the Navy staff from the U.S.S. *Williamsburg*, the Presidential yacht that Eisenhower placed in mothballs after he took office because he felt it was a needless expense. Hagerty had the questions lined up that were likely to be asked by the correspondents and he and I and the rest of the staff would figure out how they could best be answered. It was easy enough to anticipate from the recent developments in world news what questions we could count upon and, if the reporters were planning to bring up something special, Hagerty usually heard about it in advance through his private pipelines.

We were back upstairs at our desks soon after eight o'clock and Eisenhower was usually already in his office unless he had a breakfast appointment with a member of Congress or another government official, which would keep him a little later. Ready for him when he arrived were the latest State Department, CIA, and military intelligence reports, and the staff secretary, at first General Carroll and later General Goodpaster, would be on hand to give him the essentials in all the various intelligence information. Once a week the White House staff was briefed by the CIA and at the weekly National Security Council meetings the President listened to another summary of top-secret world developments by Allen Dulles, the CIA head. Eisenhower glanced at several newspapers every morning but the one more often at the top of the pile was the New York *Herald Tribune*. He paid little attention to the newspapers that continually belabored him, such as the St. Louis *Post-Dispatch*, and seldom read the Washington papers. He once said to me, "If you want to find out how the people feel about things, read the papers, but not the New York or Washington papers."

Although he was interested in histories of the Civil War and occasionally relaxed in the evening with a paperbound Western story, Eisenhower was not much of a reader. He was impatient with the endless paperwork of the Presidency and always tried to get his staff to digest long documents into one-page summaries, which was sometimes next to impossible to do. He seldom exchanged written memoranda with me or with the Cabinet members or his staff. He preferred to get his information from talking with people who knew the issues involved in the matter he was considering. He listened intently, keeping the conversation brief and to the point with no wandering digressions, and he interrupted now and then with a quick and penetrating question that brought the whole discussion into clearer focus.

Eisenhower disliked using the telephone. The only person in the government who spoke to him frequently on the telephone was Dulles, who consulted the President constantly on foreign policy matters that required an immediate decision. It was understood that other Cabinet officers and agency directors with questions for the President would come to his office rather than call him on the telephone. Now and then, when Eisenhower was at his farm in Gettysburg or on a golfing vacation in Augusta, I would telephone him to let him know of a vote by Congress on a bill that was of anxious concern to him or to schedule an appointment that had to be attended to, such as a decision on the defense budget which Humphrey and Dodge had requested. If I had to telephone him on government business, it was always something that he could answer with a brief "Yes" or "No." One of the very few times that I ever received a phone call from Eisenhower that had nothing to do with affairs of state was one summer day when he was at Newport. I picked up my telephone in Washington and, after he had disposed of a small item of business, I was astonished to hear him ask, "Are your eyes blue?" He was painting a portrait of me from a colored photograph in which the color of my eyes was indistinct.

On rare occasions I was called on the telephone by an official abroad who sought Presidential guidance. Early one morning just as I arrived at the office the White House operator called me to say that a call was waiting from far away in the South Pacific. It was the most distant telephone call I had ever received. Picking up the phone, I heard the voice of the American ambassador at that overseas post in a state of excitement, yelling at me, "They've taken down the American flag! What'll I do?"

I was able to decipher after some patient questions that a group of natives, as a prank no doubt, had raised their national flag over our own at the embassy. I suggested he present the native flag to the local foreign minister without taking any offense, explaining the circumstances.

"That's a good idea," the ambassador said. "I'll do that. Good-by."

Eisenhower's preference for getting to work early in the morning was based on a conviction that people think better at that time of day. He was always hopeful, too, that if he could get his work cleared away early in the day, he might find time late in the afternoon to get out of doors on the golf course or with a Number 8 iron on the back lawn of the White House for the fresh air and exercise that he so vitally needed. In arranging his work, he had to allow for unexpected crises that were always interrupting his schedule. One morning in the midst of negotiating an arrangement for the truce in the Korean War, he had to turn aside, once to confer with the Cabinet about new Civil Service regulations, and again to make a decision that could not be postponed on the wheat surplus problem. Then, after returning briefly to a study of more messages from Korea, he had to meet with Senator Taft, Senator Smith of New Jersey, Congressman Samuel McConnell of Pennsylvania and Under Secretary of Labor Mashburn for a hurried last-minute check on amendments to the Taft-Hartley Act.

On Wednesday morning, the President would go over to the Indian Treaty Room in the old Executive Office Building for his press conference at ten-thirty. At ten o'clock sharp, after he had finished with two hours of appointments and pressing business, Hagerty and I, accompanied by key staff people, would go into his office to go over with a fine-tooth comb the subjects that were likely to come up in the press conference. If we expected the correspondents to discuss scientific developments or atomic tests, for example, we asked Dr. James R. Killian or Lewis Strauss to attend the pre-press conference meeting. Hagerty would state a probable question and the one in the group most qualified would talk about how it could best be answered. The President said to me after one such briefing session, "I don't really need prompting from you fellows on these questions, but it's well for me to listen to you because you might point out some angles that I might otherwise overlook."

When Hagerty, with his principal assistant, accompanied the President to the press conference, none of the White House staff members tagged along behind them to watch the show. Eisenhower did not approve of that. He wanted his people to be at their desks, working, when there was no real need of their presence elsewhere. But Eisenhower did ask me to sit in on all of his important meetings and, when I could, on office appointments with government officials and with visitors where important decisions were to be discussed. He did not invite me to his meetings specifically to make any comments, although I was always free to do so if I had anything to say. On many occasions I listened until I thought the meeting had lived out its usefulness, and then I arose as a broad hint that the participants do likewise. Invariably they did. Eisenhower merely wanted me to hear everything that was going on so that I would become as familiar as possible with his attitude on most of the passing problems. I was then to use this knowledge in making decisions for him in the matters that he left for me to resolve.

It took a while for some members of the Cabinet and other high-ranking government executives to accept me as a spokesman of Eisenhower's viewpoints but, after I had served a year as his assistant, the President himself, at least, felt that I had reached that position. At that time I had an opportunity to return to private industry at a much more attractive income, and that necessarily opened up the question of my leaving the White House. I talked to the President about it, reminding him that he had often urged us to speak up if an opportunity came along that we felt, for our own economic security, ought not to be turned down. "I shall have to think of someone who can take your place," he said quickly. "During the time you have been here you have established yourself in the confidence of the Cabinet. Anyone coming in to replace you would need the time to do the same—that is," he added as an afterthought, "unless we can find someone who is already in that position. I can't think of anyone right off except possibly Cabot Lodge. I'll have him in for a talk." After a day or two, Eisenhower called me in. Lodge was happy with his work at the United Nations. He told me afterward that he enjoyed his post as Ambassador to the U.N. more than anything he had ever done. In my own mind I was sure that Lodge, if he could help it, would have nothing to do with scrubbing the administrative and political back stairs as I was doing at the White House. "So I guess you will have to stay here," the President concluded with a grin. I forgot my economic security and stayed on as Assistant to the President for another five years.

It was impossible, of course, for me to sit in on all the meetings and office appointments that Eisenhower wanted me to attend; I had too many telephone calls, too much paperwork, and too many appointments at my own office, as well as a White House staff to supervise. Somebody who made a count of such things once estimated that my outgoing and incoming telephone calls were usually 250 a day and that figure was probably not far from right. Because Eisenhower disliked talking business on the phone, Persons and I and a few other staff members would speak for him on the telephone on many matters that required his personal attention.

A considerable amount of my time on the telephone was spent on personnel problems with Cabinet members and Republican leaders, and with Eisenhower's advisers in professional and business life, gathering and listening to suggestions about filling a particular position. Then, after boiling the list down to a handful of the most attractive eligibles, I sought the President's preference. I never had the slightest hesitation in interrupting Eisenhower at his desk, or after work, for a decision that took only a brief "Yes" or "No." Whether he was at his desk or taking a swim in the White House pool or even, on occasion, in his bedroom, I was expected to come in when and if I decided it was necessary. Needless to say, the reasons for disturbing him in his private residence had to be urgent indeed. I remember that once when I needed a decision on an appointment I went out on the back lawn, where Eisenhower was practicing golf shots. Dulles was already there ahead of me on a related errand. The President saw me coming and with a simulated sigh said, "Look, Foster, here comes my conscience!" After the President had looked at the list and made his choice, I was back again on the telephone; to the Special Counsel to initiate an FBI investigation; to Charles Willis, or later Robert Gray and Robert Hampton, to follow up with clearance with the Senator concerned and the National Committee; at the proper time to the man himself to find out whether he could be persuaded to move to Washington. Eisenhower seldom if ever offered anybody a job personally. It was wrong, he felt, to put a person in the embarrassing position of being forced to say "No" to the President of the United States, and, of course, it was also embarrassing for the President to have his personal request turned down. With top-flight businessmen, the chief difficulty was getting them to work for the government at all. It was not so much the financial sacrifice and the personal upheaval in being transplanted to Washington as it was the facing up to the hazards of adjustments in public service. Government ought to be run more on business principles, they said, but the politicians always were getting in the way, and they didn't want anything to do with politics.

Despite all the telephone calls, the checks and the clearances, an occasional appointment would bounce back to haunt us. I thought I had seen to all the necessary preliminaries in the President's nomination of Tom Lyon, who had been highly recommended by Secretary of the Interior Douglas McKay and Senator Arthur Watkins of Utah for the position of Director of the Bureau of Mines. But the nomination of Lyon caused an uproar in the Senate when the examining committee heard Lyon himself say that he had no respect for the mine safety program that he would have been required to administer. That gave John L. Lewis an opportunity to shout forth in round and solemn syllables and forced the annoyed President to withdraw the nomination. I don't know yet how McKay and Watkins could possibly have overlooked this rather basic flaw in Lyon's qualifications but I had to share with them the glory of the fluff.

No matter how hard we struggled during that first year of Eisenhower's Administration to put the best possible people into the places of the higher-ranking holdovers from the Roosevelt and Truman regimes, there was a steady rumble of criticism from the politicians of our own party. We weren't cleaning out the Democrats fast enough. Too many of our appointees were from New York and the Eastern seaboard and not enough of them were Taft men. I can honestly say that Eisenhower never bothered to find out whether a prospective appointee had supported him at the 1952 Republican convention. He knew which of his Cabinet members had been for Taft but beyond that small circle I doubt if he could have passed an examination on the past party loyalties of most Republican job seekers. Soon after he went into office, Lodge gave him a brief typewritten list of names of extreme right-wing Republicans who had been violently opposed to him and advised him to give them a wide berth. Lodge added that not only had they done their best to sink Eisenhower when he was a candidate, but some of them had contributed to his own defeat by John F. Kennedy in the Massachusetts Senate race in 1952. Eisenhower added one more name of his own choice to the list in longhand and handed it to me one day and forgot about it. He made no prohibition to me about the people on the list, for, as he said, he had no personal acquaintanceship with most of them and he certainly did not anticipate that those particular Republicans would have any inclination to work in his Administration anyway. Actually there was no ground for the talk of the Administration's alleged discrimination against Taft Republicans. Along with Ezra Taft Benson, Eisenhower appointed to his official family as Presidential assistants two prominent Taft men, I. Jack Martin and Howard Pyle.

When I was being pressed to come up with a recommendation for the Veterans Administration, I decided, more or less as an experiment, to see if I could find a candidate who would satisfy the two main qualifications that we were accused of neglecting—a Taft adherent from the Midwest or the Rocky Mountains. I noticed a statement in a Washington newspaper attributed to a Republican leader in the Senate that a Taft man couldn't get over the White House threshold. There was a steady chant of such complaints, the most vocal from the National Committee, that the East or California seemed to be providing too many of our sub-Cabinet and agency appointees. With these criteria, and without departing from Eisenhower's high standards of fitness, I began my hunt. After prolonged inquiries in the middle of the country, I discovered Harvey Higley, a Wisconsin businessman who had the backing of Tom Coleman, leader of the Taft forces in that state. Higley was subsequently approved by Eisenhower and confirmed by the Senate and proved to be an able administrator. But it had taken six months to fill the job.

Behind Eisenhower's continual battle with the Republican politicians over patronage was his insistence that the Cabinet and agency heads should assume final responsibility for choosing their own subordinates. He went through well-publicized motions of transferring patronage responsibility from me to Leonard Hall in the spring of 1953, but at the same time he reassured the Cabinet that this merely meant that Hall and the National Committee would be allowed to recommend candidates for open positions. Hall's candidates, however, would get no more than equal consideration with other candidates. Dulles refused to let the Republican party have too much say on State Department job appointments because he felt that he had to depend on Democrats in Congress for support of his foreign programs. Ezra Taft Benson, always difficult with politicians, ran the Department of Agriculture with little regard to any preferred status for Republican job applicants. Charles Halleck once arranged for a group of Republicans in the House to talk with Benson about farm problems. As the men were sitting down, one of them mentioned that Truman Democrats were still controlling the Department of Agriculture's field offices in North Dakota. An argument on patronage broke out and lasted for the rest of the meeting. The farm problems were never discussed.

Eisenhower was exasperated by the time that was spent on patronage wrangles at his weekly meetings with the Republican legislative leaders. "I'll be darned if I know how the Republicans ever held a party together all these years," he said after one such session. "This business of patronage all the time—I'm ready to co-operate, but I want, and we all want, good men." At one meeting that Senator Taft attended shortly before his death, Eisenhower mentioned the difficulty he was having trying to find the right person for an important job. "He doesn't have to be a general," Taft remarked. "We have enough of them around here already." Knowland recalled that during the Truman Administration Republican Congressmen were shown the courtesy of being consulted about job applications from their districts. They had been receiving no such consideration, he added darkly, since the Republicans had taken over the White House.

Philip Young, Eisenhower's Civil Service Commission chairman until 1957, was a special target of the patronage-seeking Congressmen. In 1949, Truman had given Civil Service status to hundreds of thousands of government employees who had entered the federal service without examinations during the national emergency period in 1941 and early 1942, before and after the attack on Pearl Harbor. Halleck introduced a bill that aimed to vacate all jobs held by Civil Service people who had not taken examinations, but Young opposed the measure because of the widespread confusion it would cause and because of the damage it might do to the Civil Service system. At a legislative leaders' meeting, Congressman A. L. Miller of Nebraska told Eisenhower that he should fire Young. The President, trying to keep his temper under control, said to the Congressman, "Mr. Miller, I love to have your advice, but when it comes to picking my assistants, *I* pick them." As a matter of fact, Young was one assistant who had been picked by Eisenhower personally. After the post had been turned down successively by several well-qualified candidates, not knowing where to turn next, I asked Eisenhower if there was anybody he could think of, something that I rarely had to do. The Civil Service chairmanship was a position of Cabinet rank, regarded by the Rockefeller Committee as a crucially important command post in the government. Eisenhower immediately thought of Young, an experienced young man who had worked as a government administrator during the war and then dean of the Graduate School of Business Administration at Columbia. It was an inspired choice that made me wish I could go to Eisenhower with all of my personnel problems. Young not only had an impressive background—he was the son of Owen D. Young—and the right talents, but he was ready and able to come to Washington right away and his approval by the Senate only took ten days, a near record. Few appointments went through that smoothly.

Lunch at the White House, like breakfast, was a working meal. I usually asked my secretary to invite some Republican Senator or Representative with a problem, so that I and the staff member chiefly concerned with it might help with this particular task in congressional relations. The chief trouble with this idea was that there were not enough lunches to cover all of the members of Congress who had problems to present to the White House.

At other times I invited Cabinet or agency heads to lunch so that some item of business could be taken up and disposed of, usually with other staff members present. We also spent lunch hours going over the piles of requests for Eisenhower to speak at dinners and conventions, some of them for dates two years away. I set up what I called a calendar committee, composed of Stephens, Hagerty, Hauge and other principal staff members, who met periodically to shake down the recommendations which we would make later to the President. Stephens prepared a mimeographed list of them, which we studied and discussed, declining most of the invitations and putting some on a tentative list. When a Presidential speech had been prepared by the staff writers, I called this same staff group together for a thorough study and discussion of the draft before it went to the President. This was part of my routine staff work.

In spite of all the pressures on the President to make speeches outside of Washington, a third of those invitations that he did accept were selections of his own choice and not the result of any outside pushing. Of those that he was persuaded to make, the ones that made him wince were the purely political ones. He did not mind quite so much making speeches that were politically inspired but given before nonpartisan audiences. They were probably the best political speeches he made. A typical example was the address the President made to the Future Farmers of America at Kansas City late in 1953. The invitation came to the White House through Ezra Taft Benson, whose policies even in that first year of the Administration were already under fire, much to the distress of the Republican politicians in the farm belt. Leonard Hall, then the Republican National Chairman, came in to ask me to help him. "Can't we get the President out there to make a speech?" Hall said to me. "They'll listen to him but they are getting down on Benson."

I told Hall that I would see what I could do, and immediately summoned the indispensable Hauge and a few experts from the Department of Agriculture to see if we could work out a plan for a speech. In this instance we agreed to steer clear of any partisan approach and work in a world peace theme stressing the contribution of the American farmer. A few days later we met again to study the first draft of the writing and decided that the slant was right but it needed better brushwork and stronger treatment. So it was agreed that I should call a farm expert in Des Moines and ask him to come and help.

In preparations like this, Eisenhower would not know about the plans in progress. Indeed, until an acceptable working draft had been prepared and tentative plans drawn up by myself and the staff, he would not want to know. I found early in the game that Eisenhower expected anyone who proposed a speech to him to have the reasons for making it thoroughly thought out, a draft on paper and the trip phased into his calendar so that it did not disturb other commitments. "What is it that needs to be said?" Eisenhower would say. "I am not going out there just to listen to my tongue clatter!" Hall and I and the rest of the staff learned that we had to have a finished draft in shape and in the President's hands at least two weeks before it was to be delivered so that he could put it into his desk drawer and brood over it at his leisure. The preparation usually meant days, sometimes weeks, of staff work. Since, in the meantime, anything could happen to change the picture, we learned to keep our own counsel until we had plans in apple-pie order. Then Hall and I, probably with Persons and Hague, would tell Tom Stephens that we wanted fifteen uninterrupted minutes with the President. Before such a conference took place, Hall, Persons and I would decide who was going to carry the argument. If I was chosen to take the responsibility for the project I would start out by telling Eisenhower the purpose of our appointment and ask Hall, in the example I have cited, to sum up quickly the state of affairs in the farm belt.

"We thought you might like to go out to Kansas City for the Future Farmers convention," I would say to Eisenhower. "Benson thinks this is as good a forum as there is, and it is the younger group that we have been trying to reach. You have been intending to have a look at the plans for the Eisenhower Library at Abilene. You could leave after Cabinet that morning, go to Kansas City and speak and go on to Abilene the next morning. Perhaps Mrs. Eisenhower might want to go along from there to Denver and spend the weekend with Mrs. Doud. If she did not want to fly to Kansas City she could take the train and you could both go on from there. Here's a basic draft of a speech you could give. We thought we'd leave it with you so you can look it over."

Eisenhower would glance at the speech, read a few lines, and ask a question or two about the reasons why Hall had reported such distress with the Benson farm program. "I don't believe for a minute the farmer wants the government to be his boss," Eisenhower would say, tossing the draft into his desk drawer. I knew the discussion was over and that the President wanted to mull it over. A few days later, the President would call Hauge or myself into his office. The speech would be on his desk. "This moves along pretty well," he would say, handing back the draft, "but it seems to labor too much in trying to meet a lot of picayune criticism. After all, the farmer wants to understand his role in America and in the world today. A farmer is like any other American. When he understands his responsibilities he will meet them as well or better than any other citizen. Can't we get the feel of that more into it?"

That would mean more hours of brain-racking and writing by Hauge. Finally, Eisenhower would sit down at his desk alone and think about what he wanted to say, marking up the revised draft himself and dictating to Ann Whitman the changes he was making. Once, while he was in the laborious process of straightening out a speech, he could see that the staff was somewhat nonplused in trying to find language that would suit him. Looking the writers right in the eye he said, "I have never yet had a speech prepared for me that I did not change." In considerable degree, Eisenhower was his own speech writer. When he got through with it, and Hauge had a last look, Hagerty "wrapped it up" by sending it downstairs for mimeographing and Ann Whitman typed it on a typewriter with extra-large-sized letters so that the President could read it easily while he was delivering it.

My varied duties as Assistant to the President also included the fiscal and maintenance supervision of the White House office, one part of my job that was pleasantly free from the intrigues of party politics. I soon found out that Frank Sanderson and Willliam Hopkins, who managed the bookkeeping and clerical end of the office, needed little help from me. Their service dated back to the Administration of Herbert Hoover and it mattered little to them or to the foremen of the electrical and plumbing crews whether the occupants of the front office were Trumans or Eisenhowers. Except in an advisory capacity I had little to do with affairs within the executive mansion, but when Howell Crim, the Chief Usher, and another old hand, broke the bad news about the precarious state of the electrical equipment that serviced the White House, I lost no time in taking action without any inquiry about my authority. Water seepage had made the transformers unsafe and had corroded the lead cable into the office building and there was an excellent chance for explosions in the White House and in manholes on Pennsylvania Avenue at any minute.

The problem of finding adequate office space in the White House for the President's staff was insurmountable. Truman had worked out a plan for a new office for the President but it had been rejected because it intruded too much on the symmetry of the buildings and the landscaping plan of the grounds. The staff had to be separated inefficiently, with some of their offices in the West and East Wings of the White House, making a trip through the ground floor of the President's house necessary in going from one to the other. Still others had to move into the adjacent Executive Office Building, the hideous relic that had housed the State, Navy and War departments in President Grant's Administration. We helped the situation somewhat by moving the Secret Service offices and the headquarters of the White House police, a separate branch of the Washington police force, from the East Wing to a convenient place outside the building. Shuffling around the business offices of the co-operative Sanderson enabled us to get most of the principal members of the staff into the West Wing, near the offices of the President and myself.

The White House staff, Stephens and Hagerty in particular, spent considerable time working with the Secret Service on the President's personal safety. The detailed planning that surrounds every movement of the President is precise and meticulous. Eisenhower, for example, was never permitted to paint a picture on the White House lawn, but he was allowed to practice golf shots there. Sitting or standing still before an easel, he might have been too easy a target for a marksman with a long-range rifle but golf practice was less dangerous because it kept his body almost constantly in motion. If he went fishing, Secret Service men with rods and fishing togs were stationed upstream and downstream within watching distance to see to it that nobody whose identity was not known to them went near him. On a golf course, they moved along near him through the woods and thickets at the edge of the fairways.

When Eisenhower went on a trip away from Washington, we worked out a carefully detailed trip pattern with the Secret Service agents several days, sometimes even weeks, before his departure. The trip pattern mapped and timed to the minute the exact route that the President would follow and described what he would do and whom he would be with at each place where he stopped. Before Eisenhower left on the journey, a group of Secret Service men would travel over the proposed route, visiting the airports and hotels listed in the trip pattern and examining the rooms where the President would sleep and the public auditoriums or outdoor arenas or fair grounds where he was scheduled to make appearances. They would also familiarize themselves with the identity of the local people who would be near Eisenhower at the receptions, dinners and speaking engagements that he would attend, and commit to memory the faces and physical appearance of waiters, bellboys, elevator operators, doormen, hotel managers, reporters and photographers who would come into close contact with the President. If a gate-crasher or any other unauthorized stranger turned up in a group of people around Eisenhower at any time during the trip, the Secret Service men would spot him immediately. At all hours of the day and night a Secret Service man was stationed outside of the door of the President's hotel room, with access to a nearby telephone that he could instantly use to call security headquarters in Washington in the event of any kind of an emergency. If the President was planning to occupy the room for a few days, another telephone was connected with the White House on a reserved long-distance circuit.

Large crowds always made the Secret Service men uneasy. Their most harrowing ordeal with Eisenhower that I ever witnessed was during the parade that displayed him before a huge and wildly excited mob of people in Panama in 1956. The procession moved at a snail's pace through narrow streets jammed with solid masses of humanity for as far as the eye could see, and all the way from the United States Embassy residence to the Presidencia, the shouting and screaming crowds of people of every race and color pressed closely against both sides of the open car in which Eisenhower was standing and waving. As I watched the frantic people leaning out of every window and balcony that almost overhung the little, winding, narrow street, it seemed as though some of them were near enough to touch him. The Secret Service men, moving along on foot beside the President's car, were being themselves so jostled and jammed that they would have been powerless to prevent an assassin from having a free hand. The fact that the President of Panama had only recently met such a fate further aggravated their predicament. They could only pray that nothing happened to the President and, happily, nothing did. Eisenhower never worried about his safety and regarded the elaborate precautions of the Secret Service as something of a waste of time and effort. He believed that if an assassin was seriously planning to kill him, it would be almost impossible to prevent it. One night in Denver when we were talking about it, he pointed to the fire escape outside of his hotel room window and said to me, "If anybody really wanted to climb up there and shoot me, it would be an easy thing to do. So why worry about it?"

At about six o'clock my working day at the White House came to an end. There were always some of my associates still at work at that hour, but we tried to wind up our day by then. To have tried to keep on working in the evening would have been neither good management nor good sense. Eisenhower wanted the staff to keep fit, as he himself tried to do. He always sought a little relaxation after five o'clock, but he often spent the hour before his dinner in the Oval Room office on the second floor of his residence where many of his predecessors had worked out their policies and programs in far less troubled times. Here Eisenhower often sat around informally with members of his Cabinet and staff, or with influential members of Congress such as William Knowland, Lyndon Johnson, Everett Dirksen, Sam Rayburn, Walter George, or J. W. Fulbright, or with defense chiefs, or with close friends who had some advice to give. Over a drink and a canapé, at this time of the evening, Eisenhower smoothed the road for many of his goals and legislative purposes.

SAMUEL LUBELL

Ye Compleat Political Angler

NO ONE touched the lone glass of tomato juice on the tray. As the White House waiters passed among the guests, the Scotch, rye and bourbon drinks disappeared quickly. But the solitary tumbler of tomato juice, put out perhaps as insurance against the temperance convictions or ulcers of some one of the guests, stood untouched through the evening.

The President was in good humor, greeting each guest with warm enthusiasm. Earlier in the day he had sent a message to Congress. When someone told him that several Democratic Senators had commented ruefully, "There isn't much in that we can fight," he grinned with delight, like a boy scooping in all the marbles.

It was after dinner that the political talk started. The President had seated himself in one corner of the sofa of the Red Room, with his guests grouped in a semicircle around him. There was a moment or two of awkward silence. Then someone cracked the ice of reserve by asking whether his trick knee still hurt him while golfing. After that there was no let-up in the discussion.

It was in much this simple fashion that nearly all of the now famous Eisenhower stag dinners began. The things talked about would vary with the interests of those present or with the day's events. Some of the guests who were consulted in piecing together this sketch of a typical stag dinner recall a memorable exposition by the President of France's political problems. On another evening, when Walter Reuther and George Meany were among the invited, the discussion turned into a lively debate on what free enterprise meant.

But generally through most of 1955 the President's future political intentions were uppermost in the minds of his guests, and the scene in the Red Room tended to take on the quality of a tantalizing tableau in which the drama of a whole nation was laid bare through one man's struggle between a passion for active duty and a dream of quiet retirement.

The dream would appear first. Somehow the talk would drift around to "the farm" at Gettysburg. The President would respond with an animated discourse on the charms of country life.

If any of his guests happened to be interested in farming, he might confess that he had gone into raising Black Angus cattle on the advice of friends, even though his own nostalgic preference ran to the white-faced Herefords which he had seen around Abilene as a boy in Kansas. Then he would switch to the house itself and it would be like listening to a recital of Mr. Blandings building his Dream House.

With gay humor the President would tell of the curious problems that arose when one undertook to remodel a century-old farm dwelling. Unlike the antique the Blandings bought, the Gettysburg house had been of such sturdy construction that it seemed unthinkable to tear it down. But after two wings were replaced, air-conditioning put in, and enough new plumbing installed for eight and a half bathrooms, the President conceded "it would have been cheaper to have started from scratch."

Good-humoredly, Eisenhower would laugh it all off with some comment like, "It's our only extravagance," or by remarking jokingly, "Someday I'm going to have to get a job to pay for it all." He then would explain how much the house meant to Mrs. Eisenhower. Some friends had once presented her with photographs of seventeen different homes in which the Eisenhowers had lived since their marriage—various hotels, Army quarters, even a villa in France. The Gettysburg farm was the first home which had been their own. It had given Mrs. Eisenhower the joys of picking out her own furniture, planting her own shrubs and trees, fussing over the exact shade of green for the shutters and the colors in which each bedroom was to be painted; in short, of doing all those little things that every woman likes to do.

As they listened, his guests could not help feeling that the President was no less enamored of Gettysburg than was Mrs. Eisenhower. Usually, someone would bring up the subject agitating the group.

"Mr. President, you must run for a second term," a guest would urge. "Our party needs you. The whole world needs you."

Since this same question had come up at so many stag dinners, the President's response would show an almost practiced skill. He might talk of how much less influence he would command in a second term in view of the prohibition against any President having more than two terms. Not that he thought any man ought to have a third term, but it weakened the President for Congress to know he could not run again.

Although in good health at the time, the President would warn, "Don't rely on any one man." The Republican party had to be built around young men—"young in spirit"—not around "old-timers like me."

He might go on to cite some of "the many fine young men we have in the party." The names would vary from dinner to dinner, but among those mentioned most often would be Richard Nixon, Herbert Hoover, Jr., Bob Anderson, Cabot Lodge, Charlie Halleck, Harold Stassen, and Clifford Case. Sometimes he would top off the list by adding, "and some of the people right here tonight."

The guests would nod agreement to this accent on youth, but would argue back that "youth needs inspiration" and "you are the leader the young people of the country will follow."

And so it might go through the evening, with those present protesting Eisenhower's indispensability and the President parrying their compliments, without saying either "yes" or "no."

To most of his guests the ease with which the President left them pleasantly guessing seemed evidence of little more than political dexterity. His closest intimates, though, knew how deep ran the emotional conflict beneath the gay banter.

When World War II ended Eisenhower confided to close friends, "I've had all the glory I want. I'd like to live out my days as the head of a small college, doing some farming on the side." Actually, he became head of a rather big university. Still he never really was happy in the postwar years.

As one intimate recalls, "He was all frustrated inside watching how things were going in the world and not being able to do anything about them. He didn't regain his serenity until he became President."

To those who knew him best the rambling talk of Gettysburg was evidence of a renewal of this old conflict between a soldier's desire to exchange the rootlessness of public life for the quiet countryside, and the restless drive of a man of whom one close friend observed, "Maybe it's his sense of duty, but there is a passion in him that requires his being in the decisive center of things, giving his all."

Eisenhower's heart attack may have resolved this conflict; perhaps not. Still, this account of a typical stag dinner is worth pondering for the clues it yields to one of the more intriguing mysteries of the Eisenhower Presidency—how a general who had never run for public office before and didn't even vote until he was fifty-eight years old could be transformed, within three years, into one of the most masterful politicians in American history.

Much of the public, of course, does not even think of Eisenhower as a politician. In my interviews with voters around the country, it was not unusual to hear him praised for being "clean of politics" or criticized as "just a soldier who lets the politicians tell him what to do." Some voters even term him "a pretty good Democrat." Many see him as "above both parties."

In part, this widely held image of Eisenhower as a five-star babe in the political woods reflects an extremely narrow definition of a politician as someone who is constantly running for office or managing the campaigns of other candidates. If, however, one defines "politics" in its broadest sense—as the art of governing people through other people—there is little question that Eisenhower must be rated as a highly skilled professional, as compleat a political angler as ever fished the White House.

Both as Supreme Allied Commander during the war and as NATO's commander Eisenhower had to exercise varied political stratagems to cajole the Allied governments into co-operation. Similarly, the atmosphere of his Presidency has not been that of an uncompromising leader, defying what the public or his political associates might think. On the contrary, it would be difficult to cite any President, including both Roosevelts, who has been more adept in "giving the people what they want," or who has been more of a "party" man in patronage matters and in building a party organization, or even, considering how wide was the cleavage at the outset, who has done so well in bridging the rifts within his own party.

These being partisan times it may be worth stressing my own belief that considerable political skill is an absolute essential for an effective President. Myth makers like to make our heroes appear as demigods of perfection, ignoring that in any country with so many clashing interests only rarely is a straight line the shortest distance between two political points.

Moreover, the very affection in which the President is held emphasizes the importance of a candid examination of his role as a political leader. The deep anxieties that were stirred by his illness revealed the remarkable degree to which the American people have identified themselves with him. But how much of the Eisenhower Presidency mirrors the man and how much was contributed by the people themselves? Unless we understand the process by which the man and the people became one, both the public and his successor will be sorely handicapped in carrying out the tasks which will remain after Eisenhower has left the White House.

Perhaps it is too soon to attempt a definitive portrait of Eisenhower. Still, from talks with more than a dozen of his aides, four qualities emerge which, when tossed together, make up the recipe for what might be termed the Eisenhower magic political mix.

First, perhaps his strongest single characteristic seems to be a driving determination to win. Partly this reflects the sheer intensity with which he throws himself into everything he does, whether it be work or play. As one aide has observed, "The President doesn't even sign his name quietly."

While discussing something with a member of his staff he twirls his eyeglasses. Usually after a few minutes he is out of his chair and pacing the room. He seems to relax by turning from one form of intense concentration to another, as when playing golf or bridge.

Biologically, in other words, Eisenhower appears to have the temperament of a "free running horse," who is in constant need of working off an excess of nervous energy. Yet he also has developed a conscious discipline which enables him to exhibit unending patience when trying to conciliate conflicting viewpoints. Sometimes during such sessions he may grind his teeth, a tell-tale sign of repressed impatience. His famous outbursts of temper also seem a means of relaxing inward tensions. As one frequent target of such outbursts has noticed, "He goes up like a rocket and comes down as fast. He frets over small things and resents criticism but on big things can be as calm as a rock."

Coupled with this intense energy is Eisenhower's military training, which leaves little place for a loser. A revealing interchange with the press occurred in London shortly after he was named Supreme Allied Commander. A spokesman for the correspondents had assured him they would do anything necessary to win the war, within the bounds of truth and accuracy. Eisenhower replied, quite properly, that while he would deal fairly with his associates and Allies, he would lie, cheat, steal—do anything—to beat the Germans.

Politics is a less mortal struggle than war, of course, and Eisenhower has publicly cautioned his fellow Republicans against forgetting that "our greatest enemy is not the Democrats" but "the Communists." Still, he definitely relishes a hard-hitting political campaign—when the Democrats are the target.

After the 1954 elections some Democratic leaders in Congress protested that the tactics which had been employed by Vice-President Nixon reflected on their patriotism. Eisenhower's private reaction to these protests was, "Nixon must have done a good job if the Democrats complain so much."

Washington correspondents have often pictured Eisenhower as shrinking from the things politicians are called upon to do. Yet, his aides agree that no matter how much he has fumed or grumbled in the privacy of his office, in the end he usually has gone along with what his political advisers felt needed to be done to win.

In 1954 he actually campaigned more extensively than any previous President had in a mid-term election—although this may be credited to a bit of mislaid research. When the campaigning question first came up, Eisenhower asked Leonard Hall, the Republican National Chairman, "What have other Presidents done?"

Without thinking, Hall replied, "Oh, they all stumped for their party."

Back in his office, Hall ordered some research into the question. When completed, it showed that virtually no President had ever done much in the way of mid-term campaigning.

After the election, at a breakfast session with some Republican Congressmen, Hall related what his research had shown, remarking, "Mr. President, that was one report I never showed you."

Eisenhower's second distinctive quality is his practicality. One can comb his speeches in vain for evidences of the brand of idealism which inspired the Atlantic Charter and "The Four Freedoms," or Woodrow Wilson's League of Nations. "Enlightened self-interest" is a favorite Eisenhower phrase in justifying our foreign policy. He is apt to emphasize the point by citing our dependence on raw materials imported from abroad.

His idealism appears to find its main outlet in such personal acts as churchgoing and in a sense of duty to a cause higher than himself. His intimates have learned that no appeal will move him more deeply than "This is a duty you owe the American people." When he was being pressed to run for the Presidency, one aide recalls that every possible argument and pressure was employed upon him, "but the only one that made any difference was that it was his duty."

In carrying out this duty, though, Eisenhower is coldly logical and realistic. This combination of an idealistic sense of duty implemented by practical means can be extraordinarily effective politically. Often, in fact, it may yield much the same end results as cynical maneuvering.

That, of course, was the criticism hurled against Eisenhower during the North African landings for dealing with Admiral Darlan, the notorious Vichy collaborator. To Eisenhower, though, the issue at stake was the intensely practical one of which French leader could halt French resistance and reduce American casualties—an attitude which was supported fully by both President Roosevelt and Winston Churchill.

Again, it is not generally known that Senator McCarthy offered not to ride into Wisconsin on the Eisenhower campaign train in 1952 if Eisenhower felt McCarthy's presence would be embarrassing. After pondering the question in solitude Eisenhower decided that the cause of party unity was too important and agreed to have McCarthy ride with him.

How to handle the Wisconsin Senator remained Eisenhower's most nettlesome political problem during his first two years as President. As one of his assistants recalls, "No other issue split the White House staff so violently." Those staff members who had been active in the Citizens for Eisenhower clubs pressed the President constantly to crack down on McCarthy. Equally strong for doing nothing were those White House aides who had to deal regularly with Republicans in Congress.

Confronted with this division within his own official family and a threatened split in the Republican party, Eisenhower did pretty much what any "practical" politician would be expected to do—he let the matter drift, assuring the more ardent anti-McCarthy members of his staff that "given time these things take care of themselves."

How wise Eisenhower was will be debated heatedly, depending on how people feel about the Wisconsin Senator. A later chapter deals with some of the deeper implications of McCarthyism. In the frame of this examination of Eisenhower as a politician, however, it is worth noting that his refusal to tangle openly with McCarthy was completely in character with his handling of the "tough ones" while in the Army.

"He will make decisions if he has to," explained one wartime aide. "But he prefers to case a problem from every angle before acting. If he doesn't like any of the proposed solutions, he can let something drag for months. He used to drive some of us crazy with his slowness in making up his mind."

Nor, in line with good military tactics, is Eisenhower given to frontal assaults upon people he disagrees with. If a Cabinet member takes a position the President dislikes, Eisenhower rarely rebukes him openly. After the Cabinet meeting however, the outspoken member may be talked to by Sherman Adams, the President's chief of staff, by Nixon or by some other Presidential assistant.

One aide who has watched this "softening up" technique employed repeatedly attributes the tactic to the fact that "Eisenhower likes people and tries not to hurt anyone." But others in the White House say quite bluntly, "The President is as skilled a maneuverer as the Army has produced."

Certainly it can hardly be coincidence that while Eisenhower is popularly pictured as the grinning image of goodwill, his staff chiefs—both Bedell Smith and Sherman Adams—have been portrayed as ogres of toughness.

The third key to Eisenhower's political effectiveness will be found in a strong sense of organization. In politics an "organization man" usually is someone who has worked himself up from lowly precinct levels and who has learned to vote a straight ticket almost as a religion. Eisenhower's own party affiliations were sufficiently nebulous for many Democrats, including President Truman, to want to run him for the Presidency. Being a general, though, Eisenhower regards it as axiomatic that no commander can function without a supporting organization. As a result, he probably has been more co-operative with Republican leaders on organization matters than any previous President.

Eisenhower has invited Leonard Hall to at least one Cabinet meeting to discuss the importance of patronage for the future of the Republican party. Beyond insisting that persons nominated to the posts be qualified, Eisenhower generally has gone along with the patronage requests of Hall and Sherman Adams.

At first Eisenhower's knowledge of organization politics was so slight he was only dimly aware of what a precinct captain was. But Eisenhower is a quick learner, particularly in picking up the lingo of anything that interests him. Not long after becoming President he surprised the businessmen attending one stag dinner by asking, "How many of you here can tell me what precinct you vote in?"

None of his guests could, of course. Eisenhower then confessed,

"I was just like you," and launched into a lecture on how important it was for businessmen to interest themselves in the grubbiest details of political organization.

Not until after the 1954 elections, however, did he acquire an all-out zeal for revitalizing the Republican organization. Some of those close to him interpreted this as indicating he had decided to run for a second term. Others thought he wanted to build a strong enough organization so the Republicans could win without him.

Whatever the motivation, with characteristic intensity Eisenhower began demanding "a Republican party worker in every precinct in the country." Some veteran politicians tried to explain that no party has ever been able to recruit enough precinct workers to reach down to the last precinct. But the President brushed aside their objections impatiently. After one such session one aide walked out of the President's office muttering, "He thinks if the Army can be organized down to the smallest unit, a political party can be."

Told that a party chairman in some state was not too efficient, Eisenhower would retort, "Get rid of him. Get someone who will work." Since state chairmen are elected within the states, changing them is not quite so simple a matter. Still, by the summer of 1955 two-thirds of the forty-eight state chairmen were persons who had been named since Eisenhower became President.

At the 1952 Republican convention Senator Taft had the support of ninety-three of the 193 delegates from the Southern states. In nearly all these states Taft leaders no longer are in control. In Alabama, for example, the Taft leader was given a Federal post which, under the Hatch Act, disqualified him for political activity and opened the way for an Eisenhower man to move in. The 1956 convention will be recorded as the first public demonstration of how effective an organization steamroller the Eisenhower forces have fashioned.

The fourth ingredient in the distinctive Eisenhower political mixture is a remarkably acute sense of public relations. Here, as well, his Army training has served him well. At West Point the tactical textbooks emphasized that a good commander always visits his troops to inspire them to fight and Eisenhower has applied this lesson to Republican party workers. While stationed in the Philippines for three years, he also served as a ghostwriter for General Douglas MacArthur, who was not unaware of the political facts of life. Eisenhower was selected for the post of Supreme

Commander in Europe by George Marshall, who liked his generals articulate and who, himself, was a shrewd publicist.

As Chief of Staff, for example, Marshall made it a rule never to appear before a congressional committee or a press conference with a written statement—a tactic Eisenhower has often utilized. As Marshall liked to explain to the officers under him, "You lose much of the impact of conviction when you talk from a press release. A Chief of Staff ought to know his business well enough to answer any questions a Congressman or newspaperman might ask."

But where MacArthur and Marshall were both quite formal in their approach to the public, Eisenhower is the epitome of informality. All his aides agree, "He has a natural gift for doing the right thing." During a tour of New Hampshire the Eisenhower party was having dinner at the home of Sinclair Weeks, the Secretary of Commerce. Weeks had planned on serving charcoal-broiled steaks, but the open-air fireplace would not draw properly.

Eisenhower, who delights in demonstrating his culinary ability, waved Weeks aside and, with the aid of a cook and another servant, fixed the fireplace and proceeded to broil steaks for everyone.

The next morning, as the Eisenhower party was about to drive off, the President ejaculated, "I forgot to say good-by to my friends in the kitchen!"

Jumping out of the car he dashed back into the kitchen to shake hands with the cook and servant who had helped him with the steaks.

Such warming gestures, invaluable in American politics, come spontaneously. Still Eisenhower has a lively appreciation of the value of his own personality. In discussing what moves people to vote he has remarked, not boastfully but as if stating an objective fact, "Think how many votes that 'I like Ike' slogan was worth to us."

The President has his grumpy days. Tom Stephens, his former secretary, noticed that on such days Eisenhower usually wore a brown suit, which led to these off days being referred to in the White House as his "brown suit mood." Basically, though, Eisenhower is an optimistic person. "I've never heard him say that something couldn't be done," recalls one aide. Eisenhower rarely misses an opportunity to try to infect those around him with this "nothing is impossible" feeling.

His heavy reliance on personal charm is also apparent in the impressive number of persons he has entertained in the White House. The guests at his stag dinners alone had passed the twelve-hundred mark by the summer of 1955. He had also lunched or breakfasted with nearly every member of Congress at least once and with some hundreds of Republican functionaries.

Eisenhower has developed the politician's knack of calling a person by his first name on a second meeting. He will refer to even slight acquaintances as "my friends." One person who watched Eisenhower at a gathering with Congressmen observed, "He's a great one for cottoning up to someone who's been giving him a little trouble. He'll do everything but embrace the man."

Some of his critics have tried to picture Eisenhower as being manipulated by Madison Avenue advertising agencies, citing such actions as his efforts to improve his television delivery by calling in screen star Robert Montgomery. But this charge misses the essential point, which is Eisenhower's complete readiness to use every kind of publicity appeal.

Once one of his aides remarked casually that the American people had never seen a Cabinet session in action. The next day Eisenhower had Jim Hagerty, his press secretary, working on the idea of televising the Cabinet.

Again, Eisenhower co-operated wholeheartedly with the effort to swing the 1954 elections by a last-hour appeal to ten Republicans to phone ten other Republicans in chain-letter fashion urging them to vote. The persons Eisenhower telephoned were selected with all the care of a TV give-away program. His mail for three weeks was gone through. The likeliest prospects among the letter writers then were interviewed personally to make certain they would publicize well. Through the whole telephoning stunt Eisenhower was as relaxed as if talking to old friends.

The many facets of Eisenhower's political character are not easily summed up. But the more important faculties are revealed perhaps in Eisenhower's oft-expressed admiration for Oliver Cromwell, who, as Eisenhower once told a G.O.P. pep rally, "sent his Roundheads into battle singing hymns and chopping off the heads of their foes." In his own approach to politics Eisenhower has managed to combine Cromwell's zeal to win and sense of a Heaven-bound mission with a keen sensitiveness to the psychological intangibles that make for good organization and effective public inspiration.

One further aspect of Eisenhower's evolution as a politician should be noted. Although the qualities we have cited were part of the man all along, it took him almost two years to learn how to apply them.

At the start of his administration some of his aides felt "he was frightened to death of politics." This fear apparently was transmitted to the White House staff. In those early months virtually everyone in the White House seemed to have two dominant concerns. One was to say nothing publicly—the President had made clear he would crack the military whip on possible "leaks." The other was to avoid stubbing their political toes, particularly in dealing with Congress.

One person who worked with some of Eisenhower's key aides at the time recalls, "I never heard anyone defend a proposal by saying it was the right thing to do. All the talk centered around what was politically smart."

This period of fumbling by "too many political cooks" tended to fade as the President's confidence in his own judgment grew. What impressed his staff most as they came to know him was his remarkable energy and intellectual curiosity. When a new problem arose he would press questions on even minor details with the avidity of a student cramming for an exam. Nor would he rely on his staff alone. Through stag dinners and visitors he would search out other opinions. Often after such conversations his aides would get a note from the President demanding, "What about this?"

But the real turning point in his political growth seems to have come with the change in his relations with Congress. These hit bottom during the spring of 1954. In drafting his 1954 State of the Union message Eisenhower had put forward what he and his staff considered a "bold new" program of what the Republican party should stand for. He had called for a liberal foreign-trade program and continued foreign aid, a tax structure to stimulate consumer and business spending; also a four-year public housing program calling for thirty-five thousand units a year, liberalization of the social security system and the expansion of health insurance by guaranteeing private insurance companies against loss.

Instead of organizing to put through this program, however, the Republican leaders in Congress made the Bricker Amendment the first order of business. Then came the Army-McCarthy tangle. By spring the President's program seemed virtually forgotten. Pacing his office angrily, Eisenhower would demand of his aides, "What does the Republican party want to do—commit suicide?"

As the 1954 election drew near, however, many of the Republicans in Congress were reminded that they would need Eisenhower's support in the campaign. Congressmen and Senators began drifting into the White House to have their pictures taken with the President.

Politicians are like women in that nothing improves their morale more than a little courtship. With a sense of his own political appeal quickened, Eisenhower's spirits perked up. Then came the cheering evidence that the famed Eisenhower "luck" was still working.

Instead of being weakened by the Democrats' winning control of Congress in the 1954 election, Eisenhower found his own position strengthened. Freed of having to rely on the so-called "right wing" of his own party for legislative support, he acquired a new maneuverability. The closeness of the 1954 election also convinced him that the public supported his "middle of the road" program.

By the spring of 1955, as one assistant recalls, "the President was feeling that he was a hell of a good politician." Not long before his heart attack, in talking with friends he remarked, "I know what the people want and my program gives it to them."

During the French Revolution a foreign ambassador was lunching with one of the Revolution's leaders when a mob came tearing by. Leaping to his feet, the leader hastily excused himself. "I must catch up with that mob," he explained. "I am their leader."

That legendary anecdote is worth bearing in mind in any appraisal of the Eisenhower Administration. Eisenhower was elected in 1952 to fill a deeply felt need for leadership. Many persons saw him, in the words of one elderly widow in Jacksonville, as "the man God always sends this country in time of need." Some cynically sophisticated observers credited his victory to a Freudian yearning for a "father image."

But if the Eisenhower landslide reflected a widespread desire for a hero who would hoist a standard and proclaim, "Follow me," that is not what Eisenhower has done. On the contrary the essential quality of his leadership has lain in the skill with which he has followed the public mood. Like our French mob leader, he has led the people by moving in the direction toward which they were already inclined.

Such a pattern fits neatly, of course, with Eisenhower's own belief in the warmth of conciliation. Early in his Presidency, when many commentators were urging him to get rough with Congress, he would protest to intimates, "Some people think that to be a leader you must pound on your desk and show people who is boss. But that's not my way of working."

But perhaps more important than personality has been one impersonal fact—an acute consciousness, shared by the whole White House staff, that the G.O.P. still is the minority party in the country.

To friends, Eisenhower has repeatedly voiced his determination to do everything possible to restore the Republicans to their old position as the majority party. Eisenhower has done things which he knew would cost the Republicans votes, as with his veto of the pay increase for postal workers. Still, few administrations have given more thorough attention to the political effects of their actions or have been more zealous in courting the public.

Perhaps the best evidence supporting this conclusion will be found in the faithfulness with which Eisenhower's more important policies have reflected the desires of the electorate. One can turn back to the 1952 election and find, in what people said and felt as they voted for Eisenhower, a virtual outline of what later became the Eisenhower policies. What is more, the conflict which tore at the emotions of the voters in 1952 still defines the choices between which people's voting is being pulled today.

ERIC F. GOLDMAN

The Crucial Decade and After

NO FEAR OF CONSERVATISM

JUST AS the Administration was getting fully under way headlines reported the physicians' bulletins. March 4, 1953: STALIN GRAVELY ILL AFTER STROKE. March 5: STALIN SINKING: LEECHES APPLIED. March 6: STALIN DEAD. Within days the new premier, Georgi Malenkov, was making speeches about solving all "troublesome and unresolved questions . . . by peaceful negotiations." With a rush of hope the American public asked: Did the end of the tough old dictator mean the end of the Korean War?

During his postelection trip to Korea, Eisenhower had become convinced that continuation of the stalemate was intolerable. The one major remaining issue between the U.N. and the Communist negotiators was whether the more than 22,000 North Korean and Chinese prisoners of the U.N. who said they did not want to go home would be forced to return. Nothing had seemed to be able to break this deadlock, including a proposal made to the U.N. by India in November, 1952. Prisoners unwilling to be repatriated, New Delhi urged, should be supervised by a commission made up of Poland and Czechoslovakia, both Communist, and Sweden and Switzerland, both neutral, and a fifth nation to be named. The mildest comment any Communist leader made about the plan at the time was Andrei Vishinsky's "unacceptable, unsuitable, unbelievable." Eisenhower agreed with Dulles that the Communists should be told that the new American policy was: Peace or else. The Administration would continue to negotiate sincerely. But if the stalemate went on, the United States would fight to win, and this meant air attacks beyond the Yalu and the tactical use

"No Fear of Conservatism" and "The Eisenhower Equilibrium," following, are from *The Crucial Decade and After—America 1945-1960* by Eric F. Goldman (pp. 243-257 and 267-279).

of atomic arms. The Secretary of State undertook to see to it that the Chinese thoroughly understood the American position. He explained it personally to Prime Minister Nehru of India—a man with decidedly good communication lines to Peiping.

In 1956 Dulles expressed his belief that the American threats broke the deadlock in the truce negotiations. Other experts have argued that the prime difference was the willingness of the new Soviet regime to permit an armistice. Indian spokesmen have pointed to their proposal, maintaining that it provided a sensible solution which the Communists ultimately recognized as sensible. Whatever the reason or reasons, things happened in early 1953.

On February 22 the U.N. commander, General Mark Clark, had written the Communists another in a long series of letters urging that something be done about exchanging sick and wounded prisoners. He did not receive a reply until March 28 but he was startled at its contents. The Communists were not only ready to arrange such an exchange; they wanted to discuss "the smooth settlement of the entire question of prisoners of war." Truce negotiations which had been given up since the fall were resumed, the sick and the wounded were exchanged, and the conferences moved toward peace. By June 17 a settlement seemed close.

But the postwar remained the postwar, endlessly productive of jarring news. That June 17 the Associated Press carried eighteen special bulletins in the day period, sixteen in the night report, and for one twenty-minute period news came in so fast that nothing was put on the trunk wire except flashes. East Berlin, restive after Stalin's death, broke into open revolt. Supreme Court Justice William Douglas stayed the execution of the convicted atom spies, the Rosenbergs. Near Tokyo a C-124 crashed in the worst air tragedy up to that time, killing 129 soldiers and airmen. And 78-year-old Syngman Rhee, determined that there should be no truce except one which united Korea under him, capped all the bulletins with an act of utter defiance.

At 2 A.M., June 18, Dulles was awakened by the ringing of a telephone in the bedroom of his Washington home. An officer at the State Department was calling to say that Rhee's soldiers were cutting through the wire compounds and freeing thousands of North Korean and Chinese prisoners. Dulles listened quietly, grunting an occasional "yow" and trying to shake off the sleep. As he reached over to switch on the light, he broke through the heaviness and realized that the United States was close to major fighting, perhaps on the verge of a nuclear World War III. Wouldn't the

Communists now walk out of the peace conference, bringing into effect the drastic measures which he and Eisenhower had agreed upon? "This is as critical as June, 1950," the Secretary believed.

Dulles picked up his direct phone to the White House and had the President awakened. Both men were ready to go ahead. The bombing targets beyond the Yalu had already been carefully picked so as to limit them to areas of indisputable military importance.

But the Communists really wanted a truce. Their representatives stormed and they sulked but they went right on negotiating. Soon the final papers were ready. The military demarcation line was fixed near the 38th parallel. (South Korea gained 2,350 square miles of North Korean territory and North Korea added 850 square miles south of the 38th parallel.) The forced repatriation issue was settled approximately along the lines of the Indian proposal. During the months of bitter negotiations each side had made important concessions. The U.N. had not gained acceptance of an inspection system trustworthy enough to make sure that preparations for another attack did not go ahead in North Korea. The Communists, although they won face-saving amendments to the original Indian proposal, were denied forced repatriation.

Promptly at 10 A.M. on Monday, July 28 (it was 9 P.M. Sunday, July 27 in Washington) the two senior negotiators entered the little truce building at Panmunjom—the mild-mannered General William K. Harrison, tieless and without decorations, and the bristling North Korean, General Nam Il, sweltering in a heavy tunic sagging with gold medals. Aides carried back and forth nine copies of the main documents (three each in English, Chinese, and Korean) and the two men sat at separate tables, silently writing their signatures. By orders of Syngman Rhee, no South Korean signed. When Harrison and Nam Il had finished, they rose and departed without a handshake or a word.

After thirty-seven months and two days the war that was never officially a war, which had cost America alone 25,000 dead, 115,000 other casualties, and twenty-two billion dollars, was over. The U.N. and the U.S. had stopped aggression; they had neither won nor lost the war. They had managed to arrange a truce; the truce was as flimsy as the bitterness of Syngman Rhee or the plans of the Communists might make it. They had established emphatically before the world that Communist advances could be resisted. They had not necessarily contributed to anti-Communist feeling in pivotal Asia.

Along the front lines U.N. soldiers heard the news broadcast in nine languages, smiled and yelled a bit but mostly stood around talking quietly. Once in a while somebody would grin and say something like: "Don't forget where you put your gun. You'll need it next week." General Mark Clark told reporters: "I cannot find it in me to exult at this hour." Foreign correspondent Dwight Martin cabled back that many top U.S. military men in Korea were perfectly aware of the arguments that freedom had been defended and aggression repelled but took little joy in the truce. "They all seem concerned," he added, "that some day they will be called on to explain why they signed the present armistice. Several I've talked to specifically think in terms of investigating committees demanding to know whether it is a fact that they sold out Korea. They frankly admit that complex justifications and explanations, currently acceptable, may look pretty lame in a year or so."

The evening of the armistice President Eisenhower appeared on television solemn-faced. He spoke of his relief that the killing had been stopped but he quickly added that what had been gained was "an armistice on a single battleground, not peace in the world. We may not now relax our guard nor cease our quest." Here and there in the United States celebrations started up and quickly petered out. In Philadelphia a soldier who had already managed quite an evening tried to keep things going. He went up to a man standing on the corner. "Wonerful, ishn't it? Jus' plain dern wonerful."

The man hailed his cab and paused for a moment. "I don't know whether it's wonderful, son. But anyhow it's over."

The removal of the specific pressures of the Korean War permitted the Administration to develop more rapidly its general defense and foreign policies. In part they sprang from a strategic calculation—that there was no longer any one year in which the danger of war was greatest but that policies must be laid down to take care of a number of years, any one of which might be critical. But more basically the change came from an impatience at the Democrats' dependence on the policy of containment, with its huge year-after-year expenditures for armament and for economic aid to other countries, its tremendous concern for the opinion of allies, and its assumption of the necessity for adjustment to a worldwide social revolution that would probably go on for decades. The Republican policies were heavily influenced by the Taftite insistence on economy and the Taftite skepticism that talk of adjusting to a world social revolution was just so much more global New Dealism.

The basic decisions were made in late 1953 and summarized in a speech which Secretary of State Dulles delivered before the Council on Foreign Relations on January 12, 1954. The Administration, the Secretary said, was aiming for "a maximum deterrent" of aggression at "a bearable cost." To achieve this, it was going to de-emphasize "local defense" and rely more on "the deterrent of massive retaliatory power . . . a great capacity to retaliate, instantly, by means and at times of our own choosing." Instant retaliation by means and at times of America's own choosing—the United States was not going to be too concerned about the attitude of allies. Less dependence on local defense—the United States was going to cut down expensive ground forces and rely more on air power and atomic weapons.

In line with the policy of massive retaliation the Administration took what Admiral Arthur Radford, chairman of the Joint Chiefs of Staff, called a "New Look" at the defense budget. It trimmed $2,300,000,000 in expenditures and $5,247,000,000 in defense-spending authority from the Truman proposals for the fiscal year 1954. At the same time the Administration was taking a new and skeptical look at the whole policy of economic aid abroad. A raft of statements came from officials which gave credence to the report that Eisenhower would propose cutting off all economic aid by June 30, 1956.

The new defense and foreign policies, particularly the massive retaliation speech, provoked strong and sustained opposition. Adlai Stevenson, dropping his banter, solemnly charged that the Administration was putting dollars before defense and threatening the unity of the Western world. Within the Administration itself General Matthew Ridgway, a member of the Joint Chiefs of Staff, fought the whole trend so hard that he brought about some amendments to the plans for cutting the ground forces. But for the most part the Administration stood its ground and with a way of arguing that emphasized the heart of its policies.

At the heart was restlessness, the restlessness of generations of Americans at having to deal with a strange and unruly world, a restlessness enormously magnified by the exasperations and fears of the post-World War II period. The massive retaliation speech was essentially another declaration of peace-or-else; it probably marked, as the strongly pro-Eisenhower historian Merlo Pusey has commented, "the zenith of the cold war." A dozen speeches implied that the United States was not willing to settle for containing Communism. We were going to be "positive," the President said. He had not given up his policy of "liberation," Dulles added. Cantankerous allies as well as Communists were not to be dallied with indefinitely. The French, the Secretary of State made plain, could bring about "an agonizing reappraisal of basic United States policy" if they did not do as America wanted and join the European Defense Community. And always there was the traditional American assumption that only a few evil leaders stood in the way of a world-wide acceptance of American values and hence of peace.

"What we need to do," Dulles declared, "is to recapture the kind of crusading spirit of the early days of the Republic when we were certain that we had something better than anyone else and we knew the rest of the world needed it and wanted it and that we were going to carry it around the world."

On Capitol Hill Senator Joseph McCarthy was asked his judgment of the new Administration and he smiled loftily. The Administration's record on anti-Communism, he said, was "fair."

Circumstances were hardly such as to curb the arrogance of Joseph McCarthy. The Republican capture of the Senate in 1952 had made him for the first time the chairman of his own committee —the powerful Committee on Government Operations—and he also headed its formidable subcommittee, the Permanent Subcommittee on Investigations. With a handful of exceptions the whole Senate treated him with respect or at least with care. He seemed to have proved what a politician respects most—an awesome ability to affect votes. He himself had been re-elected in 1952 by a majority of more than 140,000. No less than eight of the men in the Senate—six who had been elected in 1952—were thought to owe their seats largely to his campaigning. Around the country his name had an increasing potency. A belligerent if small pro-McCarthy faction was making itself heard even among the group which had shown the most solid bloc resistance to him, the intellectuals of the United States.

Probably most important of all, the man in the White House had a conception of his role which very specifically ruled out openly battling McCarthy. Eisenhower not only wanted to respect the Constitutional division between the executive and legislative divisions. He was keenly aware that he was the head of a divided party and anxious to unite it along the lines of his own thinking. Whatever the President's own tendencies toward the right, his views were quite different from those of the right-wingers, who for the most part were bitter anti-New Dealers, all-out isolationists with respect to Europe, all-out interventionists with respect to Asia, and enthusiasts for the kind of anti-Communism represented by McCarthy. These men followed the President reluctantly when they followed him at all and Eisenhower wanted to do nothing to increase the friction. It was the President's "passion," his aide C. D. Jackson remarked, "not to offend anyone in Congress" and this attitude soon permeated most of his subordinates.

Month after month McCarthy went to further extremes and month after month the Administration sidestepped, looked the other way, or actually followed his bidding. At the beginning of the Administration McCarthy declared that he believed there were still Communists in the State Department and that Dulles could go a long way toward rooting them out by naming a good security officer. The Secretary named a good security officer—Scott McLeod, widely assumed to be a McCarthy disciple. March, 1953, and the Senator announced that he had negotiated with Greek shipowners to stop trading at Soviet and satellite ports. Director of Mutual Security Harold Stassen angrily pointed out that this was a flagrant Senatorial interference with the functions of the Executive Branch and that by negotiating with a small group "you are in effect undermining and are harmful to our objective" of stopping the general trade with the Communists. Immediately a mollifying statement came from Frank Nash, Assistant Secretary of Defense for international affairs, and Secretary of State Dulles and McCarthy got together for a congenial lunch. At his press conference, the President did the final smoothing over by suggesting that both McCarthy and Stassen had gone a bit far. The Senator had probably made a "mistake" and the Director of Mutual Security probably meant "infringement" rather than "undermining."

All the while McCarthy was stepping up his campaign against the State Department's overseas information program. The country began to hear about the two 27-year-olds, Roy Cohn, the Subcommittee's chief counsel, and G. David Schine, an unpaid Subcommittee consultant. They left on an eighteen-day whirl through western Europe to ferret out "subversion" in the overseas program. Seventeen hours in Bonn, twenty hours in Berlin, nineteen hours in Frankfurt—these and a sprinkling of other stops and McCarthy was proclaiming "appalling infiltration." The State Department reacted dutifully. It asked for resignations—including those of men like Theodore Kaghan who had probably dabbled with radicalism in the late 1930's and who now was known through central Europe as one of the most effective organizers of anti-Communist propaganda. (When the Subcommittee made its charges Leopold Figl, the ultraconservative former Chancellor of Austria, wrote Kaghan: "What goes on? After all, April Fool's day has long passed by. . . .") The State Department also issued a new directive banning from American information activities all "books, music, paintings, and the like . . . of any Communists, fellow travelers, *et cetera*" and ordering that "librarians should at once remove all books and other material by Communists, fellow travelers, *et cetera,* from their shelves and withdraw any that may be in circulation."

Many librarians, taking no chance on having a work by an *et cetera* on their shelves, removed the books of authors like Bert Andrews, chief of the Washington bureau of the Republican *New York Herald Tribune;* Walter White, head of the anti-Communist National Association for the Advancement of Colored People; Richard Lauterbach, former European correspondent of *Time*; Clarence Streit, chief figure in the strongly democratic movement for a federal union of the North Atlantic democracies; and Foster Rhea Dulles, a decidedly anti-Communist professor at Ohio State and cousin of the Secretary of State. Some librarians stored the books they removed; others burned them.

At the height of the book purge, on June 14, President Eisenhower went to Dartmouth to receive an honorary degree. Among those sharing honors with him were his friend John J. McCloy, Judge Joseph M. Proskauer of New York, and Lester B. Pearson, Canadian Secretary of State for External Affairs. The President overheard these three discussing with horror the book burnings and joined in the conversation. When he rose to make his extemporaneous remarks, Eisenhower said: "Don't join the book burners. Don't think you are going to conceal faults by concealing evidence that they ever existed. Don't be afraid to go in your library and read every book as long as any document does not offend our own ideas of decency. That should be the only censorship.

"How will we defeat Communism unless we know what it is? What it teaches—why does it have such an appeal for men? . . . We have got to fight it with something better. Not try to conceal the thinking of our own people. They are part of America and even if they think ideas that are contrary to ours they have a right to have them, a right to record them and a right to have them in places where they are accessible to others. It is unquestioned or it is not America."

Anti-McCarthy opinion in the United States was jubilant. At last the President was taking a stand; now the Senator would have the whole prestige and power of the Administration thrown against him. Many papers were like the *Baltimore Sun* in calling the Dartmouth remarks an "important turning point."

The day after the speech Secretary Dulles met his regular press conference and reporters quickly got around to the book purge. Yes, books had been burned, Dulles said, but after all they were only a small number of titles among the more than two million volumes in the libraries.

But didn't the President's speech indicate a new policy? the newsmen asked.

No, just the use of more sense in applying the directive, the Secretary of State replied. As the reporters pressed on, Dulles abruptly changed the subject.

On June 17 Eisenhower met the press for the first time since his Dartmouth speech. He was asked if he intended the remarks to be "critical of a school of thought represented by Senator McCarthy." The President replied that he must refuse to talk personalities. The speech was not a stand in favor of using Government money to propagate Communist beliefs. He was against book burning, which to him meant a suppression of ideas.

No, he had not ordered any directives canceled, although he had asked Dulles to see him about the problem. He really didn't know much about the whole matter.

A newsman asked about the "controversial" but non-Communist books. The President replied that if they were on the shelves of libraries in this country, it was all right to have them in our libraries abroad, generally speaking. Then Eisenhower added that if the State Department was burning a book which was an open appeal to everybody in a foreign country to be a Communist, then he would say that the book falls outside the limits in which he was speaking. The State Department could do as it pleased to get rid of such books.

For two weeks reporters harried Eisenhower for clarification. At one press conference Raymond Brandt, chief Washington correspondent for the *St. Louis Post-Dispatch,* questioned the President sharply and at length. Eisenhower was having trouble keeping his temper as he answered.

Brandt: "Do you and Secretary Dulles hope to get a clear directive [about overseas library policy] eventually?"

The President: Well, certainly.

Brandt: "Is that possible?"

The President: Certainly, he hoped that it was.

Brandt: "Is it possible?"

The President: It should be; yes, it should be. There was no question as to where he stood. Now, he thought we could make it clear so that any reasonable person could understand exactly what was meant.

Brandt: "I think there was some confusion between your Dartmouth speech and your press conference speech in which you said it was perfectly all right for the State Department to burn books or do as they pleased with them."

By now the President was glowering. He snapped back that he didn't believe he said that. He said that the Government would be foolish to promulgate and help to support the distribution of a book that openly advocated its own destruction by force.

Brandt: "One of the writers was Dashiell Hammett, who writes detective stories. So far as I know—and I have read several of them —I don't see anything Communistic about them, but they were thrown out by the libraries. . . ."

Eisenhower smiled and his composure returned. He thought someone got frightened, he said. He didn't know why they should —he wouldn't. He would tell them that—he wouldn't. And there the discussion ended.

McCarthy rampaged on. With the opening of 1954 he and his staff concentrated increasingly on the Department of the Army and a number of top Army officials tried hard to work with them. In January the Senator began to hammer on the case of Major Irving Peress, a New York dental officer. Peress had been permitted to receive his regularly due promotion and granted an honorable discharge after he had refused to sign an Army loyalty certificate and after he had refused, on the grounds of possible self-incrimination, to answer a number of questions at a Subcommittee hearing. In a letter to McCarthy, Secretary of the Army Robert Stevens acknowledged that the Peress case had been mishandled and stated that if he found the promotion had been anything but routine he would discipline the officers involved. He also ordered that in the future Reserve officers who refused to sign a loyalty certificate were to be given an other than honorable discharge.

Unappeased, the Senator summoned Peress and a group of

Army officials, including Brigadier General Ralph Zwicker, to a Subcommittee hearing. At one point, when the hearing was in executive session, McCarthy demanded that Zwicker answer questions concerning the processing of the Peress case and Zwicker replied that such information was inviolate under a Presidential order. The Senator was furious. According to Zwicker, McCarthy shouted at the General: "You are a disgrace to the uniform. You're shielding Communist conspirators. You are going to be put on public display next Tuesday. You're not fit to be an officer. You're ignorant."

Zwicker was a highly esteemed officer who was obviously simply following orders. The Army seethed with resentment. Secretary Stevens heatedly accused McCarthy of humiliating Zwicker and of undermining Army morale, and ordered two officers not to appear before the Senator's Subcommittee. McCarthy promptly replied that Stevens was an "awful dupe" and summoned the Secretary himself to testify. Stevens decided to go and prepared a strong statement which he intended to read at the hearing. But the statement was never read. Instead Stevens met with McCarthy and other members of the Subcommittee and accepted a "Memorandum of Agreement." When the memorandum was released few commentators, pro- or anti-McCarthy, interpreted it as anything but complete and abject surrender on the part of the Secretary of the Army.

That afternoon the White House was filled with glum discussions of ways to do something about the Stevens debacle. In the Capitol a reporter passed by the hearings room of the Subcommittee, noticed the door open, and looked in. He saw McCarthy and Roy Cohn sitting at the end of the table and "laughing so hard," the newsman remembered, "that the room seemed to shake."

THE EISENHOWER EQUILIBRIUM

EVER SINCE the beginning of the 1952 campaign, Dwight Eisenhower had frequently used the term "middle-of-the-road" in describing his approach to public affairs. His Administration up to the winter of 1953-4, with its restrained Executive leadership, its toleration of extreme right-wing Republicans, its tendency toward the past in domestic and foreign policies, had certainly moved down the right side of the middle. But even in the most conservative days of 1953-4, other elements were present in Eisenhower's thinking.

All the while that he was emphasizing that the Executive should respect Congress and pointing to Roosevelt and Truman as men who had tried to lead too much, the President liked to repeat some remarks made by his old friend, General George Patton. One day Patton was discussing leadership and his eye fell on a plate of spaghetti. Leadership was like trying to get a piece of spaghetti across a table, Patton said. Push it and you would only break it. But get a bit in front of the piece of spaghetti, pull it gently, and you would get it across the table intact. Dwight Eisenhower, however much he was a leader who wanted to keep the Republican Party intact, nevertheless was quite conscious of the importance of getting out ahead a bit and pulling gently.

The President's attitude toward specific domestic and foreign problems also had its varying aspects. He was, as he frequently remarked, "basically conservative." But it was just as true to say that he was—and more so than any President in recent American history—generally non-ideological. Eisenhower tended to look for an *ad hoc* solution to a given situation and was willing to listen sympathetically to quite contrasting points of view. If he was inclined to believe that a successful businessman had thereby proved his sagacity, he deeply admired his younger brother Milton ("Milt inherited all the brains in the family"), whose mind had been shaped by years of high New Deal and Fair Deal positions.

Any policy in any field had to stand the test of the President's persistent tendency to react less along the lines of doctrine than according to the human aspects of the problem. The journalist Stewart Alsop has recalled an incident of the 1952 campaign. At first Eisenhower was strongly inclined to make a major issue of what seemed to him the excessively pro-labor attitude of Truman in dealing with a serious steel strike. Before committing himself, he asked to be briefed on the facts and some of his labor advisers explained the demands of the union in terms of what the benefits meant to the men's families in a period of rising prices. Eisenhower's reaction was, "Why maybe they ought to have had more than that," and the steel strike never became an important campaign issue.

Around the President were a group of men who were also "basically conservative," most of them more so than Eisenhower, but they had their own flexibility. All of the principal aides had spent their mature careers learning to operate within a New Deal-Fair Deal society. A number of them had served in specific functions for a Democratic Administration. This was particularly true of Eisenhower's chief adviser on foreign affairs, Secretary of State Dulles, who had worked with the State Department during most of the post-World War II period and who played a part in bringing about the highly untraditional decision to intervene in Korea. The two most influential advisers in domestic and defense matters, Secretary of the Treasury George Humphrey and Secretary of Defense Charles Wilson, were decidedly not businessmen of the 1920's type. They were part of the new, more adaptable managerial class.

In 1948 Wilson, wearied by the struggles between General Motors and the United Automobile Workers, had invented the famous "escalator clause" (tying wages to the cost of living) which labor liked so much and which was important in preserving industrial peace in the following years. In 1947 Humphrey demonstrated a similar flexibility. Facing a coal strike, he and Benjamin Fairless of United States Steel met with John L. Lewis for private talks and brought about a settlement largely on Lewis's terms. Many industrialists and a large section of Congress were indignant but Humphrey defended the move on pragmatic grounds, including the statement that Lewis's demands were largely reasonable. Discussing these episodes, the astute journalist Robert Coughlan has commented that "Wilson and Humphrey . . . have about as much resemblance to the Republican Big Businessman of the Coolidge-Hoover era as the Indian elephant has to the hairy mammoth—the general outline is the same, but there are vital differences in detail. . . . These two performances were neither 'conservative' nor 'liberal.' They were, however, practical."

Practical men, headed by an essentially non-ideological President, trying to govern a nation with conflicting urges—after the winter of 1953-4 the Administration moved increasingly from the severe conservatism of its early phase. The shift was evident in many ways, but it was clearest of all in the fact that Eisenhower was departing somewhat from his pre-F.D.R. conception of the Presidency.

He talked less and less about offending no one in Congress, left fewer major decisions to subordinates, spoke out more frequently on public issues. He was giving the appearance at press conferences that he no longer merely tolerated them but intended to use them to press forward his purposes. Only occasionally did he still remark that he just didn't know about the matter under discussion.

No one quite said it but a dozen newsmen now came close to applying to this President Bert Andrews's remark about Harry Truman after the election of 1946: Dwight Eisenhower is becoming President of the United States.

The most immediate problem facing an Executive who was genuinely trying to lead was the rampant right-wing of the Republican Party, particularly one Joseph McCarthy. A relaxing America was stirring against the extremities of the Senator from Wisconsin. As Secretary of the Army Stevens apparently yielded to McCarthy on February 24, 1954, feelings were at white heat throughout the country. Within the next ten days Adlai Stevenson bluntly called the Republican Party "half McCarthy and half Eisenhower." The Republican Senator from Vermont, Ralph Flanders, took the floor of the Senate with anger and scorn. "He dons his warpaint," the elderly Vermonter said. "He goes into his war dance. He emits his warwhoops. He goes forth to battle and proudly returns with the scalp of a pink Army dentist. We may assume that this represents the depth and seriousness of Communist penetration at this time." That night Edward R. Murrow used his CBS documentary TV show, "See It Now," for a film-clip program which was potently anti-McCarthy. CBS stations reported a flood of applauding calls (15-1 against the Senator in San Francisco and New York, 2-1 against him in Chicago).

From the day of the Memorandum of Agreement the Administration moved against McCarthy, sometimes indirectly but steadily. Secretary Stevens countered the Memorandum with a strong statement and the President made plain that he backed his Secretary "one hundred percent." On March 11, 1954 the Army attacked with the charge that Senator McCarthy, Roy Cohn, and Francis Carr, the Subcommittee staff director, had sought, separately and collectively, by improper means, to obtain preferential treatment in the Army for G. David Schine, the Subcommittee consultant who was now a private in the Army. McCarthy and "associates" promptly replied with forty-six charges against the Army, of which the key one was that Secretary Stevens and John Adams, the department counselor, had tried to stop the Subcommittee's exposure of alleged Communists at Fort Monmouth and that they used Private Schine as a "hostage" to this end. Four more days and the Subcommittee voted to investigate the Army-McCarthy clash, with TV cameras in the room and with McCarthy temporarily replaced by the next ranking Republican, Senator Karl Mundt of South

Dakota. Once again a TV spectacle would transfix the country and once again television would have a major part in shaping opinion on a critical national issue.

Shortly after 10 A.M. on April 22, 1954 the red lights in the cameras went on amid the florid Corinthian columns and the brocaded curtains of the large Senate Caucus Room. Senator Mundt tapped his big pipe, leaned forward, and delivered a little speech about how everything was going to be done with "dignity, fairness, and thoroughness." The ranking Democrat, John McClellan, said a few words to the same effect.

"Thank you very much, Senator McClellan," Chairman Mundt declared. "Our counsel, Mr. Jenkins, will now call the first witness." Ray Jenkins opened his mouth but the words came from down along the table. "A point of order, Mr. Chairman," McCarthy was saying. "May I raise a point of order?"

For thirty-six days and more than 2,000,000 words of testimony the hearings went on. A thousand impressions were driven into the public mind—Senator Mundt, roly-poly and pliable and so torn between his McCarthyite sympathies and the fact that he was supposed to be an impartial chairman that someone thought to call him the "tormented mushroom"; the Subcommittee's special counsel, Ray Jenkins, the homicide lawyer from Tellico Plains, Tennessee, chin stuck forward, intoning away with his questions; Senator John McClellan of Arkansas, the real terror of the Subcommittee, cadaverous and saturnine and pursuing everyone with a rasping logic; Robert Stevens, earnest and decent but having to pour out his, the Secretary of War's, pathetic attempts to mollify the friends of buck private G. David Schine; Roy Cohn, leaning over to make a point to McCarthy with a mouth that seemed perpetually pouting, obviously tremendously attached to Schine, obviously tremendously attached to Roy Cohn; Cohn and Schine, endlessly Cohn and Schine. But with each passing day one impression was having an increasingly potent effect on the millions at their TV sets. It was Joseph McCarthy, full-life, acting precisely like Joseph McCarthy.

"Point of order, point of order, Mr. Chairman," the Senator would interrupt in his scowling, sneering way until the children of the United States were imitating him on the streets. He repaid loyalty, like that of bumbling Senator Henry Dworshak of Idaho, by riding contemptuously over what the supporter was trying to say. He seized the floor from opponents by physical force, repeating in his strong, singsong voice until the opponent wearily gave way. McCarthy flung smears and constantly accused others of smearing; his aides tried to use a cropped photograph and he cried deceit at the Army; he sidetracked, blatantly sidetracked, and demanded the end of "diversionary tactics." Day after day he was still Joe McCarthy of the boyhood fights, ceaselessly, recklessly swinging for the knockout.

The more reckless McCarthy became, the more strongly the Administration opposed him. In mid-May the President threw the Constitution of the United States at him. McCarthy became involved in demands that were flagrant violations of the rights of the Executive and from the White House came a blunt statement of those rights, which "cannot be usurped by any individual who may seek to set himself above the laws of our land." No one, not even the President of the United States, not even a President of his own party, was immune to the Senator's standard weapon, the charge of softness toward Communism. McCarthy's answer to Eisenhower was to talk once again of "the evidence of treason that has been growing over the past twenty—" Then he paused and added darkly: "twenty-one years."

The hearings ground on. The changing national mood, the Presidential opposition, and the appearance McCarthy was making on TV were costing the Senator heavily in public support. But he was still not a ruined man. The evidence was certainly not giving either side a clear-cut victory in the issues immediately at stake. Had the McCarthy group sought preferential treatment for Schine? Clearly they had. Had the Army tried to stop McCarthy's investigation at Fort Monmouth? Equally clearly it had—though it was emphasizing that it was anxious to get "that type" of hearing ended because it demoralized the Army. Other charges and countercharges were tangled in a maze of conflicting testimony. Throughout the country a good many pro-McCarthy or anti-anti-McCarthy people were wavering but they were only wavering. The Senator could have emerged from the hearings partially intact if he had now made some moves to present himself as a reasonable, responsible person. But Joseph McCarthy was not interested in being partially intact. He went on looking for the haymaker and the right man was present to see to it that when the Senator swung his wildest, he swung himself flat on his face.

The chief Army counsel, Joseph Welch, was a senior partner of the eminent Boston law firm of Hale and Dorr and he had a well-deserved reputation as an infinitely shrewd trial lawyer. But friends emphasized more Welch's innate sense of human decency and his gift of ironic laughter. They associated him with his spacious colonial home in Walpole, where he puttered around studying his thermometers (there were twelve in the house), spending a day fishing or an evening in a game of carom or cribbage, delighting more than anything else in kindly, bantering talk about the cosmos. Mrs. Welch had a favorite story about the whimsicality of the man. She liked to tell how she had urged him to take up gardening, which he loathed, and he countered that he would garden if she would drink beer, which she detested. So on weekends the two would alternately garden in the broiling sun and stop for a beer in the shade, both grinning through their periods of suffering.

At the hearings Welch sat questioning away, his long, drooping face quizzical, his questions softly spoken and deftly insidious, dropping a damaging little jest and looking utterly surprised when people laughed. The sessions were only eight days old when the Army counsel drew blood. Welch was driving hard at a photograph which the McCarthy forces had produced, cropped to show only Stevens and Schine together although the original photograph contained two other men. The Army counsel brought out that the original had hung on Schine's wall and he questioned James Juliana, a Subcommittee employee who had arranged the cropping, as to why he had not brought the whole picture.

JULIANA: I wasn't asked for it. . . .
WELCH: . . . You were asked for something different from the thing that hung on Schine's wall?
JULIANA: I never knew what hung on Schine's wall. . . .
WELCH: Did you think this came from a pixie? Where did you think this picture that I hold in my hand came from?
JULIANA: I had no idea.

There was a stir of voices and McCarthy interrupted. "Will counsel for my benefit define—I think he might be an expert on that—what a pixie is?"

Welch's face was beatific. "Yes. I should say, Mr. Senator, that a pixie is a close relative of a fairy. Shall I proceed, sir? Have I enlightened you?"

The spectators roared. Roy Cohn's pouting lips hardened into angry lines. The Senator glowered.

In the world of Joseph McCarthy nothing was more alien than the deft, and the Senator's feelings about Welch steadily mounted. He denied the Army counsel, or was wary of giving him, what he considered the ordinary camaraderie. McCarthy would walk up to friends and opponents alike, hand extended and the other hand grasping an arm, but he moved a wide circle around Joseph Welch. He first-named almost everybody—Secretary Stevens was "Bob" and the obviously hostile Senator Stuart Symington was "Stu." Welch was "Mr. Welch" or "the counsel."

Eight days before the hearings ended, on June 9, the Army counsel led Roy Cohn through a mocking, destructive cross-examination and McCarthy sat fuming. Now Welch was pressing Cohn as to why, if subversion was so serious at Fort Monmouth, he had not come crying alarm to Secretary Stevens. When Welch went ahead along this line, McCarthy began to grin broadly.

The Army counsel got in another dig at Cohn: "May I add my small voice, sir, and say whenever you know about a subversive or a Communist or a spy, please hurry. Will you remember these words?"

McCarthy broke in, bashed his way to attention. "In view of Mr. Welch's request that the information be given once we know of anyone who might be performing any work for the Communist Party, I think we should tell him that he has in his law firm a young man named Fisher whom he recommended, incidentally, to do work on this committee, who has been for a number of years a member of an organization which was named, oh, years and years ago, as the legal bulwark of the Communist Party. . . ."

The Senator was grinning ever more broadly, pausing now and then to lick his lips and savor his words. Roy Cohn sat in the witness chair, his legs dangling apart, the blood drained from his face, and once his lips seemed to be forming the words "Stop, stop." McCarthy went on: "Knowing that, Mr. Welch, I just felt that I had a duty to respond to your urgent request. . . . I have hesitated bringing that up, but I have been rather bored with your phony requests to Mr. Cohn here that he personally get every Communist out of government before sundown. . . .

"I am not asking you at this time to explain why you tried to foist him on this committee. Whether you knew he was a member of that Communist organization or not, I don't know. I assume you did not, Mr. Welch, because I get the impression that, while you are quite an actor, you play for a laugh, I don't think you have any conception of the danger of the Communist Party. I don't think you yourself would ever knowingly aid the Communist cause. I think you are unknowingly aiding it when you try to burlesque this hearing in which we are trying to bring out the facts, however."

Welch was staring at McCarthy with the look of a man who was watching the unbelievable. The puck was gone; his face was white with anger. "Senator McCarthy," Welch began, "I did not know—"

McCarthy turned away contemptuously and talked to Juliana. Twice the Army counsel demanded his attention and the Senator talked to Juliana in a still louder voice, telling him to get a newspaper clipping about Fisher so that it could be put in the record.

Welch plunged ahead. "You won't need anything in the record when I have finished telling you this.

"Until this moment, Senator, I think I never really gauged your cruelty or your recklessness. Fred Fisher is a young man who went to the Harvard Law School and came into my firm and is starting what looks to be a brilliant career with us.

"When I decided to work for this committee I asked Jim St. Clair . . . to be my first assistant. I said to Jim, 'Pick somebody in the firm who works under you that you would like.' He chose Fred Fisher and they came down on an afternoon plane. That night, when we had taken a little stab at trying to see what the case was about, Fred Fisher and Jim St. Clair and I went to dinner together. I then said to these two young men, 'Boys, I don't know anything about you except that I have always liked you, but if there is anything funny in the life of either one of you that would hurt anybody in this case you speak up quick.'

"Fred Fisher said, 'Mr. Welch, when I was in law school and for a period of months after, I belonged to the Lawyers Guild.' . . . I said, 'Fred, I just don't think I am going to ask you to work on the case. If I do, one of these days that will come out and go over national television and it will just hurt like the dickens.'

"So Senator, I asked him to go back to Boston.

"Little did I dream you could be so reckless and so cruel as to do an injury to that lad. It is true that he is still with Hale & Dorr. It is true that he will continue to be with Hale & Dorr. It is, I regret to say, equally true that I fear he shall always bear a scar needlessly inflicted by you. If it were in my power to forgive you for your reckless cruelty, I would do so. I like to think I am a gentle man, but your forgiveness will have to come from someone other than me."

The Senate Caucus Room was hushed. McCarthy fumbled with some papers, began saying that Welch had no right to speak of cruelty because he had "been baiting Mr. Cohn here for hours."

Welch cut off McCarthy. "Senator, may we not drop this? We

know he belonged to the Lawyers Guild, and Mr. Cohn nods his head at me." Cohn was quite plainly nodding.

WELCH: I did you, I think, no personal injury, Mr. Cohn.
COHN: No, sir.
WELCH: I meant to do you no personal injury, and if I did, I beg your pardon.

Cohn nodded again. The Army counsel turned back to McCarthy and his emotion was so great that on the TV screens his eyes seemed to be filling with tears. "Let us not assassinate this lad further, Senator. You have done enough. Have you no sense of decency, sir, at long last? Have you left no sense of decency?"

McCarthy tried to ask the Army counsel a question about Fisher. Welch cut him off again. He had recovered his composure now and his voice was cold with scorn. "Mr. McCarthy, I will not discuss this with you further. You have sat within six feet of me, and could have asked me about Fred Fisher. You have brought it out. If there is a God in heaven, it will do neither you nor your cause any good. I will not discuss it further. I will not ask Mr. Cohn any more questions. You, Mr. Chairman, may, if you will, call the next witness."

For a long few seconds the hush in the room continued. One of the few rules Chairman Mundt had tried hard to enforce was the one against demonstrations and six policemen were present to assist him. But suddenly the room shook with applause. For the first time in the memory of Washington observers, press photographers laid aside their cameras to join in the ovation for Welch. Chairman Mundt made no effort to interfere and instead soon called for a five-minute recess.

Joseph McCarthy sat slouched in his chair, breathing heavily. Spectators and reporters avoided him. Finally he found someone to talk to. He spread out his hands in a gesture of puzzlement and asked: "What did I do wrong?"

Joseph McCarthy would never know. And that June day, 1954, millions at their TV sets learned once and for all that Joseph McCarthy would never know.

CHARLES J. V. MURPHY

The Eisenhower Shift

THE PRE-INAUGURAL meeting of President-elect Eisenhower and his full Cabinet and senior White House advisers at the Hotel Commodore in New York on January 12, 1953—eight days before the Eisenhower Administration took over the government—was a singular occasion in the annals of the Presidency. The gathering was to the launching of the Eisenhower economic programs what a final briefing of Army commanders had been, in the General's past, to the step-off of a major offensive. And the lid-tight secrecy imposed upon the participants was faintly reminiscent of that which surrounded the assembling of Ike's generals at Bushey Park, outside London, before the Normandy landings.

For Dwight Eisenhower himself, the Commodore session was the final transition point between an intelligent but more or less detached interest in the economic issues confronting the U.S., and an immense personal involvement in his country's economic well-being. As related in the first article of this series last month, Eisenhowever went into the Presidential campaign of 1952 with deeper convictions about economic policy than he was generally credited with, even by many of his most vocal supporters. Now, between the election and the inauguration, the admirable convictions were being applied to disagreeably specific decisions awaiting the new Administration. In these weeks "the Eisenhower shift" began—a reversal of the twenty-year trend toward more and more government influence in the economy, a shift back toward greater freedom for the individual American in his economic life.

Two subjects dominated the Commodore agenda. One was the state of federal finances. Banker Joseph Dodge of Detroit, whom Eisenhower had charged with examining the Truman books, was on hand to report on what he had found. His dismal revelations,

"The Eisenhower Shift" by Charles J. V. Murphy is from the February 1956 issue of *Fortune* Magazine.

foreclosing any realistic hope of a balanced budget before mid-1956, were reported in last month's article, together with his first forays against the inherited program of expenditures. The other subject was how and when the Administration should go about lifting the direct controls that had been imposed upon the American economy because of the Korean war. Eisenhower and his senior advisers had previously decided, during their December conference aboard the cruiser *Helena* between Wake Island and Honolulu, that the federal straitjacket on the economy should be thrown off at all possible speed. Now the intention was to nail down the broad objective by common agreement of the full Cabinet.

The Presidential group, numbering about a score, assembled in a private dining room on the main floor of the hotel. A fascinated observer was Dr. Gabriel Hauge, an economist and editor of *Business Week* who is now the economics assistant to the President. He remembers:

"It was the first time that many of us had met each other. We gathered around a U-shaped table. The President came in and while we were still standing he spoke to us briefly—nothing political, rather a humble acknowledgment of the responsibility that had been placed upon him and the rest of us, and his sense of need for the help of the Almighty. On finishing, he turned to Ezra Benson, knowing that he was an apostle of the Mormon Church, and asked him to lead us in prayer. It was an occasion of high feeling."

Ezra Benson recalls, "I didn't expect this. I was not prepared. What I said was entirely spontaneous." Taking his cue from the President's remarks, Secretary Benson called upon God to confer his blessings and guidance upon the President and his men, while acknowledging gratefully "the unselfish service of those who have preceded us, especially the Founding Fathers." Considering the stunningly bad fiscal news that banker Joseph Dodge was about to present, this was more than generous to the predecessors, excluding, of course, the Founding Fathers.

After the meal the tables were cleared, the waiters were dismissed, the doors were shut, and several hours of earnest discussion followed. Joe Dodge made his lugubrious report on the state of the national finances. Then the President called upon Sinclair Weeks, the Boston manufacturer, to present his recommendations on the removal of controls.

It is easy, three years after a decision that passed off so smoothly, to forget the profound apprehensions that surrounded the question of de-controlling the economy. The Democrats were ready to pounce if de-control was followed by any significant price rise. The labor unions were loudly fearful. Materials were still tight; many Republicans who objected in principle to direct controls were convinced that their summary elimination would touch off an explosive price rise and produce runaway inflation. Some of the President's advisers shrank from so daring an action. Here, then, with dramatic clarity, came the first sharp testing of the Eisenhower economic philosophy.

Weeks, when he rose to speak on controls, was meeting a deadline imposed by Eisenhower himself. About a fortnight after Ike asked him to be his Secretary of Commerce, a special courier had delivered to Weeks, at his Boston office, the following message:

U.S.S. *Helena*—at sea
9 December 1952

Memorandum for Mr. Sinclair Weeks:

I would like very much to include in my first message to the Congress our proposals with respect to direct price, wage and other controls. As you know, we hope to discontinue such controls as this becomes possible in favor of indirect controls which, under a sound fiscal program, are much more effective.

. . . I would like very much for you . . . to examine the situation relating to present controls of materials, wages, prices, rent, etc., and to recommend to me by January 10 a schedule for future action . . .

EISENHOWER

With the President's approval, Weeks assembled an *ad hoc* committee, which included the late Martin Durkin, the former plumber who was to be Secretary of Labor, economist Hauge, and a mixed group of businessmen and labor economists. The "general pitch" of the committee's report, Weeks recalls, was "to knock off the artificial controls and let the market go free—to give free play to the normal forces that regulate the market." Weeks and his group had carefully weighed the possible inflationary consequences. "We concluded," says Weeks, "there would be little or none."

As Weeks spoke at the Commodore meeting, and in the Cabinet discussion that ensued, two opposing views emerged. On one side were George Humphrey, "Engine Charlie" Wilson, and, somewhat less emphatically, Weeks himself ("Sinny" as the President called him), who were for de-controlling as soon as the Administration took office. On the other side was a loosely organized group who favored delaying action until about July, so as to give the economy a chance to shake down in consequence of the tremendous changes that the advent of a conservative Administration —and a possible end of the Korean war—was certain to bring. This latter group included former Senator Henry Cabot Lodge, of Massachusetts, who had been defeated for re-election two months before, and Harold Stassen; both were Republican politicians of the "liberal" persuasion and both were no doubt more sensitive then the businessmen in the Cabinet to the popular apprehensions.

There was no question of where George Humphrey stood. He recalls: "For me the big question we had to determine was how fast production would come up to supply demand. I was convinced that production operating without constraints could meet demand very quickly. The only control required in the interim was a quick tightening of credit to stop gambling in inventories."

Except for this disagreement over timing, Weeks's ideas met with the President's and the Cabinet's approval. "The President," Weeks said, "bought the report, subject to a harder look, especially as regards the de-controlling of certain strategic materials."

The harder look was started the day the Administration moved into Washington. Seeking a balance to the opinions of his businessman-administrators, the President now brought into the government an academician who had had firsthand experience with the operation of controls—Arthur Flemming, president of Ohio Wesleyan. During the Korean crisis Flemming had served in the Office of Defense Mobilization under "Electric Charlie" Wilson. Now he was summoned back to Washington as acting director of that office with the assignment of assessing the delicate timing factors in de-control.

Flemming quickly formed a partnership with economist Hauge; they in turn enlisted the help of James Brownlee, a partner of the venture-capital firm of J. H. Whitney & Co. Brownlee, a Republican, had been deputy director of Franklin Roosevelt's OPA; he possessed a deep practical knowledge of the market mechanism. Moreover, the President knew him personally and had confidence in his judgment. The independent conclusion of this trio was that the de-controlling of prices and wages could be safely started much sooner than some of the President's political advisers deemed desirable, but not quite so fast as Humphrey and Wilson wanted, and certainly not in a single stroke. Flemming and Co. were for doing the job quickly but in successive stages, so as to test the item-by-item reaction of the economy.

As a final precaution, Flemming and Hauge checked their conclusions privately with Truman's price controller, Mike Di Salle, who was still in the government. Di Salle's judgment, shared by his deputy, Joseph Freehill, was that the Republicans proposed to go too fast—the situation was explosive. That warning was disregarded. The case for the quick, stage-by-stage approach was argued by Flemming in the meetings of the Defense Mobilization Board, on which Humphrey and Weeks sat, and discussed privately by him and Hauge with the President. "Copper," Weeks says, "gave us the most worry. We took a hard look at copper. At that time it was around 24 cents and there was a shortage. At first we thought de-control might send the price sky high. Then we pretty well determined in our minds that it would probably move into the 28-to-29-cent range and so we decided that copper, too, should go into the de-controlled area."

At a Cabinet meeting on February 6, less than three weeks after his inauguration, the President decided, with a simple "Let's go," that all wage and some price controls should be lifted at once, with the rest of the price controls to come off in short order. A powerful influence in his final judgment was Humphrey's skillful advocacy of the thesis that rising production would rapidly fill whatever vacuum developed in the market and that a sharp tightening of the screws on credit would meanwhile check any serious inflationary price rise. As the Cabinet meeting was breaking up, the President momentarily detained Humphrey at the door. "I hope, George," he said cheerfully, "that you know what you're doing."

Even before the President's action, Mr. Freehill stated publicly that the killing of price controls would cost consumers $3 billion within the year. Senator Lehman of New York and George Meany, then president of the A.F. of L., both predicted the action would be "dangerous," the Senator adding "in the extreme." There were other predictions quite as dire. But on March 17, 1953, only six weeks later, the last price control—the climax of a seven-stage process—was lifted by Flemming's agency. The consumers' price index rose only slightly more than a point over the next twelve months, and the wholesale index only a fraction of a point. The one violent spasm came in copper, which, about as predicted, moved into the 30-cent range, where it stayed until last year.

In retrospect, what was extraordinary about this historic operation was not alone that it was brought off so smoothly. Its most remarkable aspect was Eisenhower's personal role: the decisiveness with which he made up his mind to proceed in so complicated an economic question, and in the face of a soldier's ingrained instinct to maintain at least a partial check on national production until the Korean war was safely disposed of. (There had been little heavy fighting in Korea since the fall of 1952, but the formal truce was not negotiated until July, 1953.) In point of fact, before the Cabinet decided to let go price ceilings on strategic materials, Eisenhower personally explored the possible repercussions on defense production; his decision was to continue *pro forma* defense-program allocations of copper, steel, aluminum, and nickel.

Supplying a new footnote to this now historic event, Flemming adds, "The key to the President's approach to the whole question of controls was his conviction that the most effective mobilization base is one resting on a strong economy. Those people who accuse us of putting a balanced budget before defense fail to understand this. What they haven't grasped is that the country is today in a strong position because the released civilian economy has created such a terrific demand that suppliers, conspicuously in aluminum, are already producing more than enough for any conceivable mobilization base."

At this stage matters were proceeding according to plan—that is, within the context of the broad objectives developed aboard the cruiser *Helena* and ratified at the Hotel Commodore meeting. With the removal of direct controls the responsibility for economic stability now rested on the indirect controls traditionally exercised through monetary and fiscal measures. This was precisely where the practical men around the President wanted the federal economic direction to rest. And now events began to propel George Humphrey, the Cleveland businessman, to the front and center of the federal stage.

Humphrey was already being marked by insiders as one of the strongest figures of the Administration. It was noted at meetings of the Cabinet and the National Security Council that the President was turning to him for counsel in fiscal and domestic matters as often and respectfully as he turned to John Foster Dulles on foreign-policy questions. Humphrey presented himself as a practical man who dealt in simple ideas: Free the economy. Cut government expenditures. Cut taxes. Return the purchasing power to the American people. They'll find more productive uses for it than governmental planners can. Humphrey's forthrightness, his flair for simple analogy, his homely habit of polarizing Cabinet discussions with the practical man's reminder, "O.K., now let's get to the meat of the coconut," impressed and delighted the President, who himself liked complicated ideas reduced to workaday metaphors.

For Humphrey the meat of the coconut was a sound dollar. He had a genuine horror of inflation and his responsibility for protecting the currency was plainly one that he took with the utmost seriousness. Entering the Treasury, he brought with him a stern resolve to balance the budget, whatever else he might or might not succeed in doing. He was plainly chagrined over his inability, in partnership with Joe Dodge, to bring down federal expenses faster. But he was preparing, in another area, a blow for fiscal orthodoxy. Men in the government were scrutinizing him closely. A Presidential adviser recalls:

"At that stage Humphrey was hardly thinking about the business cycle. He was absorbed by the urgency of getting taxes down, cutting federal expenses, checking inflation, and getting the government out of business' hair. So long as these purposes were being achieved, he could no more believe that a business contraction was possible, I am sure, than Roosevelt or Morgenthau thought one would come, as it did, in 1937."

When Eisenhower took office the economy was riding the Korea war boom. In 1952 the gross national product had soared to $345.2 billion. And after the election a bubble had attached itself to the boom. The stock market was showing an upsurge of confidence in a conservative government.

But even as Eisenhower, Humphrey, *et al.,* were settling into their unfamiliar offices, the ever fluid U.S. economy was signaling a turn. Agricultural prices were dropping: the textile industry was in trouble; foreign trade was shrinking. An armistice in the Korean war was in the offing, and the scale-down in military production that would follow was certain to impose transitional strains upon the economy.

It was Humphrey's responsibility to see to it that his anti-inflationary measures did not prick the Eisenhower bubble on the boom. Both he and Weeks knew that inventories were approaching the danger point and that these had to be liquidated. But Humphrey was confident that rising consumer demand would take up the slack created by military cutbacks, and that a "quick but moderate credit tightening to prevent price speculation" would hold the economy steady.

Humphrey's first major anti-inflationary move, on his own initiative, was the issuance in April, 1953, of the controversial 3¼ per cent, thirty-year bonds, the longest maturity on a Treasury issue since the end of World War II. This was a billion-dollar operation with subsidiary aims, including an attempt on Humphrey's part to begin shifting the public debt into longer maturities. But the main and "calculated purpose," as Humphrey says, was to tighten credit, Humphrey being convinced that inflation was still the main peril.

In the Cabinet there was no disagreement over the timing of Humphrey's bond issue. Although Eisenhower followed the discussions closely, he never seriously addressed himself to the technical points of the operation. As one of his advisers recalls, "The President today has a good working knowledge of fiscal and monetary controls, but the detailed technicalities of central banking functions, credit controls, and the like, don't fascinate him. Here he was content to trust the experts."

Humphrey's bond issue was anything but a success. The bonds were moved quickly but they soon fell below par, to a low of $98^{20}/_{32}$. Meanwhile the money market was in near-panic. Nine Democratic Senators attacked the operation as "drastically deflationary" and demanded the issue be withdrawn while a study was made of its effects on the economy.

Now came a rapid tactical fallback. The Federal Reserve's open-market purchases of government securities and its lowering of bank reserve requirements heralded a return to easier credit. And in June the Treasury turned to a short-term issue to accomplish its refunding. Interest rates started down again. The credit crisis evaporated.

Cogitating on that controversial episode, Humphrey insists that the original operation served its purpose—"exactly." He holds that "it stopped the price rise and further inventory inflation until the economy could adjust to de-controls. Then, finding we had credit a little too tight, we turned around and loosened it. If I had the same situation tomorrow, I would do exactly the same thing."

Nevertheless the maneuver, however desirable, exacted its penalty: the Eisenhower bubble had been pricked. Along with a real shortage of money, there had been a simple misjudgment of the psychology of the money market—a failure to anticipate that summary federal action would take by surprise an economy that had not yet had time to size up the ultimate dimensions of the Eisenhower anti-inflationary policies. Before long the President, who had stayed aloof from the technical controversy, found himself drawn into a far more serious situation: a distinct recession in business activity.

As the winter of 1953-54 came on—as defense production slacked off, as unemployment rose, and industry generally worked off swollen inventories—it became evident that a general contraction was in process.

Most labor economists, a Democratic opposition grouped around Senator-economist Douglas of Illinois, and even some Republican stalwarts, were sure that serious trouble was making up. And in November, 1953, their intuitions were suddenly sharpened by an apocalyptic voice across the Atlantic. Dr. Colin Clark, the Oxford economist, writing in the *Manchester Guardian*, predicted that the U.S. faced a serious depression, with six to seven million unemployed, unless the government adopted a huge spending program. Dr. Clark subsequently revised his prophecy to envisage not a prolonged trough of the 1930's type but rather a short, violent contraction—one that would require a $2-billion-a-month infusion of federal deficit spending until checked. This jeremiad was taken up by Eisenhower's critics as confirmation of their own worst fears.

At this jittery juncture a statistical reform long in preparation produced a national shock. The Bureau of the Census had ready an improved method of reporting unemployment based on a bigger sample. When the new method was applied to January, 1954, it revealed an apparent increase in unemployment of 774,000 (to a total of 3,087,000) within a single month. Although unemployment was in fact on the rise, Weeks was sure most of the increase was due to more accurate reporting. Worried, he raised the question of how the figures should be presented. The President said, "If the figures are true, put them out."

The cry of imminent disaster was picked up by the Administration's critics. Walter Reuther dispatched a letter to the President saying, "Clearly a recession has set in." From labor economists issued a spate of schemes that called for sharp tax reductions, vast programs of public works, and a variety of ingenious federal interventions.

Inevitably the fiercest pressures converged upon the President himself. A Presidential adviser remembers: "In an economic decline everybody's on the President's neck. All kinds of pressure are brought to bear—from inside the Administration and from without. Some members of the staff thought nature should be allowed to take its course. Others wanted the President to take extreme measures. Still others were for moderate, pragmatic measures. Then, too, there were pressures from business people, from labor, and from Congress."

Now began Eisenhower's first soul-searching experience in Presidential adversity, and in an area of decision where he had had no previous experience. His economic philosophy was on trial. The estimate he had to make was whether the recession could deepen into a real depression and, if so, the steps he should take to forestall that possibility. He met frequently with Humphrey, Weeks, Randolph Burgess of the Treasury, William McChesney Martin, Jr., of the Federal Reserve, and his personal economists, Dr. Arthur F. Burns, chairman of the Council of Economic Advisers, and "Gabe" Hauge.

Their consensus was that with indirect controls functioning satisfactorily the situation was inherently self-correcting. The lapsing in December, 1953, of the excess-profits tax and of the 10 per cent Korea-emergency increase in personal-income taxes, together with forthcoming cutbacks in numerous excise taxes, as well as revisions in the tax law itself, were expected, when in force for a full year, to release $7.4 billion in private spending power. Humphrey was counting upon a quick lift for the economy from this infusion, and Weeks, who was keeping a weather eye on the F. W. Dodge Corp.'s reports on construction awards, was greatly heartened by the March, 1954, figures indicating an imminent increase in construction activity.

In the meantime, however, the President was widening his own intelligence coverage. The bull sessions that were an essential feature of the White House stag dinners gave him an opportunity to thrash out, with a mixed company of labor and business executives, the broad question of what the government might and should do. However, the most interesting shift in his intellectual orientation related to the role of his economists. Prior to the onset of the recession, he had looked to his businessman-administrators for economic specifics, and their specifics had been, for the most part, well to the right of the middle of the road. Eisenhower did not get around to appointing Arthur Burns until a month and a half after entering the White House. But the conditions Eisenhower laid down for his senior economics adviser, the manner in which he quietly brought him forward at the critical point, demonstrate a remarkable intellectual resiliency—a capacity to adapt tactics to unexpected circumstances.

Burns had been a professor of economics at Columbia when Eisenhower was its president, but their only encounter there had been a perfunctory handshake at a faculty reception. In offering Burns the chairmanship of his economic council, the President said, "You've got to remember I'm a farm boy—I know nothing about economics. There are going to be a lot of politicians telling me what to do and I shall have to listen to them. So to balance them I am going to need the soundest economic advice I can get. What I'll want from you are the facts."

The President was familiar with the Council of Economic Advisers dissension-ridden career under Leon Keyserling. He warned Burns, "I want you as my adviser but I don't want to have to sit at a table and listen to a lot of talk." Burns said he was drawing up a report on how economic advice might most effectively be given the President.

"That's good," said Eisenhower cheerfully, "but I hope the report won't be too long. I can't read."

"That's all right with me, Mr. President," answered the economist. "I can't write."

In June, 1953, the President reconstituted the council under Burns's chairmanship, but with the condition that he would deal directly with Burns. At first the President had seen Burns irregularly. Then, as the business cycle turned down, he began to see him weekly, for half-hour briefings, usually in company with Gabriel Hauge. At the President's request, they also sat in on Cabinet meetings, where he could call upon them.

The President's increasingly intimate relationship with his economist is important because of the light it throws on the boundaries of the "middle of the road." In addition to the pressure to which he was being subjected by his party leadership—the narrow Republican congressional majority would be at stake in the November mid-term elections—Eisenhower was also experiencing for the first time the fierce heat generated by the professional lobbies—farm, housing, etc. Burns and Hauge were in a unique position to observe the President's response to the arguments roaring around him, and the reasoning that finally persuaded him to risk a little more sail when his more conservative advisers were still for reefing in.

Says Burns: "I was going to say that his attitude was one of impatience but that does not quite express it. He did show impatience at times. He would ask, 'Why aren't we doing something? Why aren't we doing more?' Fundamentally he wanted action but he was not so impatient that he was prepared to grasp at anything. From the beginning he stood apart from the school of thought that wanted the government to pursue a hands-off policy. The President felt it was the government's responsibility to prevent sizable unemployment. I don't know where he acquired this view but he got it somewhere. It figured strongly in his thinking and it was most encouraging to me."

Hauge thinks he knows how Eisenhower came by this idea. During the 1952 campaign, Eisenhower familiarized himself with the Employment Act of 1946—the law that authorizes the federal government to take such measures as may be required, including public-works projects, to maintain a high level of economic activity within the free-enterprise system. But whereas planners of New Deal persuasion interpret that law as a mandate requiring the government to assume unlimited responsibility for full employment, Eisenhower takes it as a moral charge on the President to do whatever is consistent with the principles of a free economy based —as Hauge puts it—on "the traditions of thrift, honest work, and self-reliance." Thus, Hauge continues:

"These basic predilections were reflected in the President's reactions during the recession. It was not in his nature to jump in with what he called 'slam-bang' emergency programs. The year 1954 was the critical year for his philosophy. Then the pressures for large-scale federal intervention reached their peak. He withstood them. It was a gamble. But the President stood firm. He concentrated on a growth program and that program did what it was supposed to do."

What Hauge calls the Eisenhower "growth program" was summed up in a series of economic messages sent to Congress during the winter and spring of 1954. These messages called, among other things, for a more liberal treatment in corporate taxation of depreciation allowances and research and development outlays, and for some relief from the double taxation on dividends; for a widening of old-age and unemployment benefits, a liberalization of housing credit; and a somewhat bigger highway program.

The President's economic advisers undoubtedly had a part in these proposals, for they are both in the "liberal" wing of the Administration; but the President himself, and especially in Cabinet discussions, was the prime mover. The "growth program" gave substance and force to his middle-of-the-road economic philosophy. It showed that the President did not shrink from moderate injections of federal money into an economy that had lost a little of its buoyancy. The "internationalist" side of his generally conservative economic outlook was even more plainly manifested in his sponsorship, in the summer of 1954, of a vast new federal highway program. That particular project—stymied in Congress but now being pushed afresh by the President—accords with his conviction that the government bears responsibility for the continuous development of common resources.

The President's steadiness, the tax reductions, the moderate enlargement of welfare programs, and of course the basic resilience and vigor of the economy itself all combined to make that overballyhooed recession of 1953-54 the mildest on record. By midspring of 1954, many of the crucial economic indicators had steadied, and by autumn the economy was heading up again. Actually the net loss to the economy was small. When the recession was at its "worst" the gross national product was running only 3 per cent below the 1953 high.

Could even that relatively modest contraction have been softened? Arthur Burns has reflected much on the event. "In 1953," he has decided, "we did the right thing. I wouldn't change anything we did that year. The Korean war was over. The right thing was to cut federal expenses. But whether we cut expenditures too fast in 1954 is debatable. In January of that year I made a forecast of the rate of spending, public and private, the economy could expect. Also, when an upturn would occur. The forecast didn't turn out badly—in the private sector. But on public spending, which should have been easy, we were wrong. In preparing the forecast I got independent estimates from experts throughout the government. Then I brought the experts together with my people and kept them in my office for two days while they went over the figures. We decided that federal spending by mid-1954 would be $2 billion less than the rate at the end of 1953. As it turned out the decline was larger.

"How did that happen? No one knows the full answer. It certainly wasn't planned that way. The Treasury, the Bureau of the Budget, the Defense Department, all were getting figures on the drop in expenditures. But nobody believed them, expecting a reversal by May or June. It didn't come."

The 1954 decline in federal spending was actually $4 billion greater than expected. The explanation of the mystery does not lie alone in the presumption that Joe Dodge's expense slashing had been more successful than anybody had anticipated. The key undoubtedly lies somewhere in the Pentagon, whose budgetary techniques—particularly the time it takes to get money spent—still baffle laymen. That strange, perhaps unnecessary plunge in defense spending, by prolonging the readjustment into the fall of

1954, may have been the miscalculation that lost the Administration its control of Congress.

Government is an open book to its critics; it is an enigma only to those who practice it. Even before the experience with the recession had registered its full impress, the President was drawn into a battle with the right wing of his party on a critical economic issue.

That battle determined the outlook for the critical fiscal year ending June 30, 1955. As related in the first article of this series, there was little that the new Administration could do about the fiscal 1954 budget situation inherited from Truman except to groan and hack at the surface fat. But fiscal 1955 the new Administration did have something to say about, and the forecast indicated a deficit exceeding $6 billion unless the President and Humphrey were able to stave off tax cuts written into the law—which many Republican Congressmen were straining not only to enforce but to enlarge.

On the principle that cuts in federal spending should precede tax cuts, the President undertook with Humphrey to seek from Congress a six-month extension (i.e., through December, 1953) of the excess-profits tax, then producing an annual revenue of about $2 billion. Unfortunately for this spartan program, seventy-seven-year-old Dan Reed, chairman of the Ways and Means Committee—the source of all revenue bills—had decided taxes simply must come down. And H.R. 1, the first bill on the docket of the new Republican Congress was one Reed had introduced himself, calling for the expiration of the 10 per cent personal income tax increase six months ahead of schedule. This threatened to cost Humphrey an additional $1.5. billion in revenues.

Eisenhower swung his personal prestige behind Humphrey's logic in an effort to win over the Republican leadership. The President personally converted Joe Martin, Speaker of the House, whose hand had been itching for the tax-cutting ax. He also turned around Charles Halleck, the majority leader. But he could not make a dent in Reed's convictions.

Unable to move Reed, the President had no choice but to snow him under. Reed's bill was buried by the device of having the Administration-dominated Rules Committee refuse to report it out. Reed retaliated by refusing to call his committee into session to discuss Humphrey's bill extending E.P.T. Toward the end of June, with E.P.T. on the verge of expiring, the Administration's sweet talkers went to work on Reed. Vice-President Nixon called upon him. So did Arthur Summerfield. The President had Reed at the White House at least twice for private talks, to no avail. Reed was finally beaten by a threat to whisk an Administration bill, planted in the Rules Committee, around his flank; and a House committee witnessed the spectacle of the old man's rising to his feet and demanding, "What have I done in my thirty-five years [in the House] that you should do this to me?"

The President thus triumphed on an issue of fiscal prudence. But, having gained his point, his magnanimity promptly reasserted itself. Reed has been back to the White House many times. He has been heard to say after such a visit, "You can't help but feel a great affection for that man."

At this juncture the President fought an equally harrowing battle with an even more formidable conservative, Senator Harry Byrd of Virginia. Ike lost. In July, 1953, the federal debt was at $272 billion and with a probable $5-billion-plus deficit by mid-1954 staring them in the face, he and Humphrey had no choice but to swallow their pre-Washington convictions and seek a quick change in the $275-billion debt limit. Humphrey wanted a margin of $15 billion for fiscal maneuvering. But when the request came before the Senate Finance Committee, of which Byrd was then a minority member but its dominant figure, it encountered a stone wall. Byrd recalls, "George Humphrey came before us and recited the facts as he saw them. He was sure the government was about to run out of money and unless we raised the debt limit there'd be a panic. I didn't agree. The President called me to the White House. Humphrey came in. He repeated his arguments. 'Harry, I've got bills to pay,' he insisted. My answer was, 'George, I've been over the situation myself and I'm just as sure you don't need the money.' "

Like Reed, Byrd was stubbornly determined to make the Administration live up to conservative tenets, whatever contortions it might have to go through in order to survive. Power over the debt limit, Byrd holds, is "the only real control Congress can exercise over expenditures." The difference is that Byrd beat the President and Humphrey in a Republican-dominated committee. The debt ceiling stayed at $275 billion.

"Well," Byrd continues, "the heavens didn't fall. There was no panic. The government met its bills." Not until the following year—and meanwhile there had been occasions when the Treasury's cash balance was equal to less than two weeks' expenditures

—did Byrd finally consent to a temporary $6-billion increase in the debt limit. And this he did, he says, only after receiving the President's personal assurance that the increase would not "be abused." "Not that I thought it would be," Byrd adds. "I just wanted to be sure."

As a result of saving the E.P.T. revenues for six months more and of an extension of the Korea increases in corporation and excise taxes, the federal deficit in fiscal '54 was only $3.1 billion—or $6.6 billion less than the 1954 Truman budget calculated. Meanwhile, in December, 1953, Dodge had ready the fiscal '55 budget, the first the Administration could call its own. That budget called for spending $65.6 billion—or $12.3 billion less than the Truman 1954 rate. By close figuring, Humphrey and Dodge thought the deficit could be narrowed to $2.9 billion. However, in consequence of the 1953-54 recession, the Treasury's income fell $2.4 billion below expectations; the actual deficit was $4.2 billion.

In the spring of 1954, with the Administration's fiscal goals tantalizingly in sight, Joe Dodge resigned, to resume his banking business in Detroit. (He has since returned to the government as a Presidential adviser on foreign economic affairs.) He was succeeded as budget director by a New York banker (National City) Rowland R. Hughes. The budget for fiscal '56, now past the halfway stage, completes the heroic task Dodge and Humphrey began.

The balance hoped for by mid-1956 now appears a certainty (with a relatively minuscule surplus of $200 million). And the imminent success is all the more remarkable for the reason that it has been brought off in the face of certain adverse circumstances that would have dismayed the President and his men, had they been foreseeable three years ago.

When Eisenhower made his famous campaign promise at Peoria in October, 1952, to balance the budget "within four years," he assumed federal spending could be brought down to about $60 billion. Now, however, the annual expenditure level has apparently stabilized at about $65 billion—that is, about where it was last year, and nearly $2 billion above the expectations of a year ago. The continuing high level of spending is due primarily to a doubling of the estimated costs of agricultural price supports and a decision to raise the annual military outlays to slightly above $35 billion (or $2 billion above the 1953 target). However, this is not to say that the "federal additive habit" of Joe Dodge's nightmare is once more gaining ascendancy. More "growth programs"—such as the expanding school, housing, and highway programs proposed in the January State of the Union Message—do indeed take money. How these programs fit into the Eisenhower economic philosophy of 1956 will be explored in next month's article. Meanwhile, the President's Peoria pledge has been saved by the tide of prosperity that has swelled the intake from corporation and personal-income taxes well above original calculations—a windfall that itself is an outcome of national confidence engendered by the President's economic policies.

RICHARD H. ROVERE

Public Law 4

Letter from Washington
February 17, 1955

IN HIS speech before the Foreign Policy Association last night, the Secretary of State did not give an altogether clear answer to the question of whether we are determined to hold Quemoy and the Matsus at all costs. He did, however, say that the Administration has not yielded to the suggestion to abandon them. This is about what everyone had expected him to say, and this is about what everyone, including people who think it would be folly to be drawn into a war over these indefensible outposts, would have wished him to say, once he had decided to discuss the matter at all. He might have said nothing about Quemoy and the Matsus, in which case the situation would be precisely what it is now, but if he had said either much more or much less than he did, he would have invited a Communist attack on the islands. His one alternative might have been an attempt at a truly candid exposition of this vexed situation and the way it is being dealt with here. Had he chosen that alternative, he would certainly have confused the Communists. He might also have confused his listeners, and even himself.

It is at this moment a thoroughly mixed-up situation, and one reason Mr. Dulles could not have made a categorical statement, even if he had been so undiplomatic as to wish to do so, is that the Administration itself has not settled upon a course. Or, at least, that is the appearance of things here at this juncture. One gets the impression that the only orders given the Seventh Fleet in regard to Quemoy and the Matsus are orders to check with Washington before doing anything drastic. One gets the further impression that the President is one member of the Administration who is determined not to go to war over the offshore islands if he can find any possible way of avoiding it. His area of choice is being narrowed, however, not only by the Chinese Communists, who have the primary power of decision at this stage, but by the pressures on him here. There is, and for some time has been, a split in the Administration that can be roughly described by saying that on the one hand there is a White House faction favoring a minimum of commitment in the Far East and a Pentagon-Capitol Hill faction favoring a maximum of commitment. This may do some injustice to the true delicacy of the situation but by and large it is recognized that the President wants out and the Joint Chiefs of Staff and Senator Knowland want in. It may turn out that these differing points of view will have no bearing on what happens in the Formosa Strait in the coming weeks, for there is little doubt that if the Communists should launch an attack on Quemoy and the Matsus that was clearly preparatory for their promised assault on Formosa, we would be at war. The differing points of view would have extreme relevancy, though, in the event of an attack that was judged by our intelligence people to be an operation of limited scope, intended to assure Peiping's security and not to destroy Formosa's. They would also be relevant in the event of a Communist offer to bargain for control of the offshore islands in return for a promise to abstain from an armed attack on Formosa and the Pescadores. That the President is open to such a proposition was shown in his call for a negotiated cease-fire, which quite obviously could not be arranged unless there was a surrender of the islands within artillery range of the mainland. Senator Knowland and Admiral Radford are opposed to any such deal.

The feeling here is that unless Peiping resolves the whole issue by making good on its threats to clobber the off-shore islands at an early date, this conflict will continue but will be settled before too long in a fairly clear-cut victory for the President. It is pointed out that although he does not wield the power of his office as forcefully as some of his predecessors, in this struggle he has won every contest so far. If Admiral Radford, who is becoming almost wistful in his repeated suggestion of a blockade of China, had had the upper hand in the last few months, it is of course possible that no one would now be concerned with weighing the prospects for peace. But in almost every case the President has pursued the exact opposite of the course recommended by the Joint Chiefs, and there is no reason to suppose that he has any different plans for the future. His independence of his military advisers has been in many ways remarkable, and quite a few people feel that he has been able to get away with it only because he is a military man himself. A civilian President who was told by his Joint Chiefs of Staff that the nation's security required a certain course of action would have to either take their advice or get himself a new set of Joint Chiefs. President Eisenhower has no need to do one thing or the other. He knows that he is at least the peer of any of his Joint Chiefs as a strategist, and if he should be disturbed by the possibility that his views are colored by his political background, he can recall the fact that the backgrounds of the present Joint Chiefs are no more innocent of politics than his. These men were more or less foisted upon him by Senators Knowland and Taft, because Senators Knowland and Taft felt that the country would benefit from having military leadership that rejected the Europe-first views of the group headed by the President's old associate General Bradley.

It is perhaps even more remarkable that the President has won most of his battles over Asian policy with Senator Knowland, for while a civilian President tends to be awed by generals, a military President tends to be awed by senators. Nevertheless, Mr. Eisenhower has usually had the better of the argument with the congressional leader of his party. There is clear evidence of this in the events of the last month. Senator Knowland did his part in seeking congressional approval of Public Law 4—the joint resolution on the defense of Formosa—and of the Mutual Defense Treaty with the Republic of China, but he did it with an unconcealed distaste for the only provisions in those documents that represented any sort of change from existing policy. These were the request for a negotiated cease-fire in Public Law 4 and what has been called the "re-leashing" section of the treaty—Article 1, in which the Nationalist Chinese signatories pledge themselves to refrain "from the threat or use of force in any manner inconsistent with the purposes of the United Nations." If anything, Senator Knowland's objections to these provisions went deeper than Senator Morse's objections to everything else in the documents, but Senator Knowland had been maneuvered by the White House into a position that forced him to accept them, in order to get a reaffirmation of principles that would have been adhered to in any circumstances —the defense of Formosa and continued military aid to Chiang. The prevailing view here, then, is that if the President weathers this crisis, he will be pretty firmly in control of policy in his own

Administration. Provided the Communists have the good sense not to press their attacks in the Formosa Strait, the case of Admiral Radford and Senator Knowland will be greatly weakened.

Even if the peace is preserved there are bound to be difficulties growing out of the events of the past month. It is almost universally acknowledged here that Public Law 4 and the Mutual Defense Treaties have created fully as many problems as they have solved. Many people, including a large bi-partisan group of the senators who voted for it, feel that Public Law 4 will haunt the executive branch of government for many years to come. For what the President did in requiring Congress to approve in advance a course of action for which he already had full authority under the Constitution was to act as if the Bricker amendment, which was narrowly defeated in the last Congress and might be narrowly passed in this one, were so sound in principle that its provisions should be honored even without its being enacted into law. The President, of course, opposes the Bricker amendment in practice, and it was not because he endorses it in theory that he asked Congress to allow him to do what he had a full right—even an obligation—to do under existing law, and what, in fact, he had been doing all along. He wanted, for one thing, to impress Peiping with the degree of unity behind American policy, and for such a purpose a congressional resolution is effective; he also wanted, it may be assumed, to share with Congress the responsibility for the large risks that were being run. "Eisenhower is passing the buck," Senator Morse said at one point, and no one, even among the Administration's supporters, took issue with him. The President was doubtless mindful of the reproach that met President Truman's failure to consult Congress before ordering air and sea support for the Republic of Korea in June of 1950. With the Communist armies slicing down the peninsula, President Truman did not have time to ask Congress to approve his action (it is unlikely that he would have done so even if there had been time), and there will be crises in the future when President Eisenhower and those who follow him will not be able to sit back and wait for the Senate, with all its pride in its tradition of unlimited debate, to grind out a resolution. But any future President who neglects to ask Congress's leave in a matter of this sort will be accused of ignoring the admirable precedent set by Mr. Eisenhower in 1955.

It is ironic that the President surrender of executive power in this case is one that Congress, normally eager for whatever it can get, would just as soon not have received. For although the President seemed to be taking Congress into partnership in the making of foreign policy, the really important thing he was after was its approval of a particular piece of military strategy. He wanted Congress to approve the Seventh Fleet's participation in the evacuation of the Tachens; he wanted it to join with him in making the threat to break up troop and aircraft concentrations on the mainland; and he wanted it to underwrite his scheme for containing Chiang Kai-shek on Formosa and the Pescadores. (This last was not part of the resolution, but it was implied in the section calling for a cease-fire to be negotiated by the United Nations.) While Congress has always treasured its right to conduct post-mortems over military decisions and to raise general hell over military blunders, it has never revealed any wish to be an accessory before the fact. It has —since the Civil War, at any rate—been altogether content to have the chain of military command come to an end at the White House, and there is no doubt that if there had been any quiet and passably ethical way of rejecting the President's generous offer of a share in the determination of strategy in the Formosa Strait and the East China Sea, Congress would have made a grab at it. But once the President had told the country what he planned to ask of Congress, there was no way out. Congress has now been made a party to strategic decisions, and this, too, is a precedent that many people here expect will reverberate down through the years.

The Mutual Defense Treaty also broke new ground. Though the majority of observers, like the majority of senators, felt that more could be said for it than against it, there was widespread agreement with Senator Morse's view that it is a most peculiar document and one that we may very well live to regret ever having negotiated. During the floor debate, the proponents of ratification made no reply to Senator Morse's contention that what was under discussion was not really a treaty at all. "I do not believe the document before us meets the legal tests of a treaty," he said. "It is not a treaty with a sovereign power." In law, as he pointed out a treaty is defined as a compact between two or more sovereign and independent nations. The Chinese signatories to this agreement represent no sovereignty whatever; they have no title to Formosa, which was wrested from Japan, after fifty years of possession, by the United States and now has the status, if it can be called that, of a *de-facto* American protectorate whose fate will some day be decided by the United Nations. The Nationalists are merely guests there. Chiang Kai-shek has scarcely any better claim to the island than General de Gaulle had to the United Kingdom when he was using it as a base of operations during the war. Mr. Dulles affirmed that this was also the State Department's view of the matter, and the Senate Foreign Relations Committee was so alarmed by the prospect of the Nationalist rulers' acquiring illusions of sovereignty from the treaty that in its report it incorporated the statement "It is the understanding of the Senate that nothing in the present treaty shall be construed as affecting or modifying the legal status or sovereignty of the territories referred to in Article VI." Article VI provides that "the terms 'territorial' and 'territories' shall mean in respect of the Republic of China, Taiwan [Formosa] and the Pescadores." Formosa and the Pescadores are geographical realities, but in the American understanding they are no part of the Republic of China, which is not a place but an idea. The Republic of China does not mean the Chinese mainland; one of the main purposes of the treaty is to prevent the Nationalist armies from touching off a war by attempting to return to the mainland. It is true that the Senate Foreign Relations Committee's expression of "the understanding of the Senate" is not part of the treaty proper—as many people feel it should have been—and thus may have no legal meaning. It is also true that the Nationalists are arguing that a resumption of the Chinese civil war on the mainland would not be a use of force "inconsistent with the purposes of the United Nations." Nevertheless, the American point of view, as expressed by both the Secretary of State and the Senate Foreign Relations Committee, is that the Nationalists have no title to Formosa, where they reside, and no business attempting to force a restoration of their authority in the mainland. In fact, the only territories to which no one here disputes their legal claim are the offshore islands like the Tachens, which we have urged them to evacuate.

"How can you sign a treaty with a government without recognizing that it has a habitation as well as a name?" Herbert Elliston, a distinguished critic of American diplomacy, wrote in the Washington *Post & Times-Herald* the other day. No one has dealt with this question. (In fact, the advocates of the treaty left almost all questions unanswered—doubtless because they knew from the start that they had the votes. The debate, especially on the Administration side, was not on an elevated plane; a fair sample of what passed for argument and fact was the suggestion made at one point by Senator Goldwater, of Arizona, that "we might start with a consideration of the massive land-attack theory of Genghis Khan and its subsequent improvement by Alexander the Great.") The answer to Mr. Elliston's question seems to be that we have entered not into a treaty, which the Supreme Court has held to be "primarily a compact between independent nations," but into a military alliance of the sort that has sometimes been made by this nation and other Western nations with nomadic chieftains. Whatever we have entered into, most people believe that, with things what they are at the moment, the alliance is to our advantage, and that, far from increasing the chances of war in the period directly ahead (as Senator Morse contends), it will decrease them. Not very many found it possible to disagree with Mr. Dulles's statement that "failure to conclude this treaty would have the gravest consequences." But some of the consequences of concluding it also seem grave. Chiang Kai-shek regards the agreement as a recognition of his authority on Formosa and the Pescadores. His state of mind does not alter the realities, but the majority of people here think that his reading of this particular document is an entirely legitimate one, and that if the issue were to be tested in international law, the language of the agreement would be said to uphold his point of view more strongly than that of the Senate. And the importance of this, as was pointed out in the memorandum prepared by Benjamin Cohen, former counsellor of the State Department, and circulated without endorsement by the Democratic National Committee, is that whatever strengthens Chiang's case necessarily strengthens that of the Communists. If Formosa is legally part of the Republic of China, and if the Republic is legally superseded by the People's Republic, then Formosa is legally part of the People's Republic. If the defense of Formosa is a defense of Chinese territory, then an attack on Formosa by the Communists would not, as the Cohen memorandum puts it, be "international aggression on their part but civil war, in which the right and purpose of other nations forcibly to intervene would be open to serious doubt and question." The memorandum adds, "What we recognize as territories of Chiang's China other countries, including our allies [who] recognize Mao's China, may feel compelled to recognize as territories of Mao's China."

There is another bit of distasteful logic that follows from the alliance. The State Department has signed what most people concede to be an advantageous contract with Chiang Kai-shek, the one Nationalist leader in whom the department has confidence. Chiang, however, is sixty-eight years old and not in the best of health. It is expected that when he dies, the struggle for the succession will be as intense and as difficult to interpret as the struggle now going on in the Soviet Union. It is more than likely that the United States will not wish to be bound as closely to the victor or victors in that conflict as it has been bound to Chiang, and this is unquestionably the reason the State Department wrote into the agreement a provision, in some ways insulting, that makes the document subject to termination on a year's notice. (Twenty years is the normal period for which we obligate ourselves by treaty.) The Chinese signatories are surely not unaware of the apprehensions that caused us to insist on the provision, but they would be derelict in their duty if they did not claim that despite the provision we are morally bound to defend not only Chinag Kai-shek but his heirs and successors in the government he now heads. It is, indeed, their duty to recall and emphasize the high-flown sentiments of the treaty preamble, which speaks of the "mutual pride" in "the relationship which brought [these] two peoples together in a common bond of sympathy," and to ask where the United States acquired the right to negotiate an understanding with a single leader or faction. Mr. Elliston, in his comment on the lack of clarity in respect to the status of Formosa and the Pescadores, quoted the British historian A. J. P. Taylor, who recently observed that "diplomacy is an art which, despite its subtlety, depends on the rigid accuracy of all who practice it." Of the treaty as a whole, Mr. Elliston wrote that it "comes perilously close to the disingenuous. It is wrong in every sense of the word if the parties to a transaction are not at one over the meaning of it."

MICHAEL STRAIGHT

How Ike Reached the Russians at Geneva

THROUGHOUT the final day at the Geneva Conference, the chiefs of state struggled to write their Directive. At five o'clock they agreed upon its ambiguous wording. And that evening they returned for what should have been a round of friendly generalities spoken in farewell. "In our Directive," declared Sir Anthony Eden, who spoke first, "we have included the essentials of a comprehensive settlement." It was then up to Marshal Bulganin to second this moderately hopeful view. Instead the Marshal read an unyielding repetition of his original demands. He spoke in a low voice, and as he spoke the Soviet delegates gripped the sides of their chairs and stared at the floor. These things must be spoken for the record, they were sorry.

Bulganin was followed by President Eisenhower. In a few dignified phrases he passed over Bulganin's challenge. He recorded once more "my lasting faith in the decent instincts and good sense of all peoples" including the Russians. Then, when the conference ended, he went over once more to embrace and to reassure the Soviet leaders. The final impression that the American experts brought away was of Bulganin, Khrushchev and Zhukov, beaming and basking in the warmth of the President's personality.

Whether the Russians needed more time to consider the proposals made at Geneva, whether they were offended by their defeats at the propaganda level, or whether they had to end on a strong note in order to bolster the satellite regimes no one knew for sure. Two things alone seemed certain on that Saturday night: the first was that the personal impact of President Eisenhower was tremendous in Geneva; the second, that the meaning of the conference would turn, as the President concluded, on the follow-through. And if it was not certain, it seemed reasonably sure that in the five days from July 18 to July 23, 1955, the world moved a short but measurable distance toward peace.

The American approach to the Geneva Conference was summarized by President Eisenhower in his opening address . . . "We cannot expect here," he said, "to solve all of the problems of the world. . . . It is out of the question in the short time available to the heads of governments meeting here to trace out the causes and origins of these problems and to devise agreements that could, with complete fairness to all, eliminate them. Nevertheless we can perhaps create a new spirit that will make possible future solutions."

In this key passage the President reconciled the irreconcilables of Geneva: the bitterness of its origins and the necessity of overcoming bitterness; the impossibilities of real agreement and the public demand that the impossible be attempted; the pessimism of Dulles and the President's view that "pessimism never won a war."

Because of its origins the Geneva Conference seemed doomed at first to fail. It was, it is worth remembering, brought into being as a means of inducing the French Assembly to ratify the German Accords. The French supposed that a conference at the Summit would lessen tensions and make German rearmament superfluous, but the reverse seemed a more likely result. The Soviet Government after all had warned, over and over, that ratification would increase tensions and end all hopes of negotiation in Europe. And while the Soviet leaders could not afford the political penalties of refusing to attend a conference dedicated to peace, they were under no compulsion to be generous at Geneva, least of all in payment for what they had described as an act of treachery.

The negative approach to Geneva was reinforced by the personal pessimism of Secretary Dulles. For twenty years the Secretary had followed each maneuver of Soviet diplomacy. He had learned to be suspicious of overtures from Russia, scornful of generalities, skeptical of agreements, and doubtful about apparent changes of heart. He dreamed that his lifetime of diplomacy would be crowned with a peace settlement. But his dreams had a way of ending in nightmares dominated by Senator Knowland. He felt that in the period of Western strength that would follow the German Accords a year of hard Yankee trading might begin to show results. And he anticipated this trading with the grim pleasure of a lawyer trying a criminal case. He granted and then appraised the propaganda advantages of making the first play for public opinion in any conference. He weighed them against the bargaining advantage in forcing his adversary to make the first move. The canny trader in him chose the second course. Above all, Mr. Dulles remembered that, thanks in part to his own talents, the good names of Franklin Roosevelt and Harry Truman had been blackened before history with the brushes of Yalta and Potsdam. With his lawyer's concern for his client and his preoccupation with domestic politics, Mr. Dulles was determined that Geneva would never serve as a brush for Democrats to blacken Eisenhower. So, at Mr. Dulles' direction, negativism was the American watchword before Geneva.

The primary objective at Geneva, as Mr. Dulles interpreted it, was not to reach a settlement with the Russians but to preserve the unity of the Allies. With this approach the working parties of the Foreign Office, the Quai D'Orsay, and the Bonn Government agreed.

And yet public opinion, taught over lean years to believe in negotiation through strength, pressed for proposals that the Russians might accept. The pressure mounted sharply after January.

Le Degel is the French title of Ilya Ehrenburg's novel *The Thaw*. And *le degel* was the phrase used with some irony by the French to describe the months that led up to Geneva. During those months the Soviet leaders thawed not only in the sunshine of garden parties but in the shadows of conference rooms. Even the coldest of Soviet officials, Mr. Molotov, thawed out enough to apologize to Secretary Dulles for repeating the old Soviet line at San Francisco. "This anniversary celebration," Mr. Molotov explained, "is neither the time nor the place for serious talks."

The foreign ministers and their experts were content to ignore the thaw until it proved to be real. Their chosen approach to the Geneva conference remained unchanged. But the chiefs of states, unlike their servants, are public figures. They are political leaders, spokesmen of the national purpose and custodians of the national morale. The public may be moved by illusions, but chiefs of state cannot rough-hew these illusions.

The world's hopes for Geneva mounted following the thaw. And, thaw or no thaw, the three chiefs of state understood that it was for them to give expression to these hopes.

Edgar Faure was the weakest of the three and also the least involved. In France, where foreign policy is peripheral, premiers are not made and broken by their record on world affairs. Faure nonetheless felt impelled to establish France's independence and his own role as an innovator in statesmanship. He lacked the political power to undertake a man-to-man appeal to Marshal Bulganin. He could not, like Eden, propose further concessions on Germany since, as an advocate of German unification his neck was already well extended on that issue. He chose therefore the Mendèsian course of an ambitious scheme relating disarmament to economic benefits through budgetary controls which, no doubt would create fascinating problems in the case of France alone. His proposal certainly caused little loss of sleep among the Russians, but Frenchmen seemed well satisfied.

Sir Anthony Eden was also thinking largely in political terms. Superficially his leadership was unchallenged in his own country. In fact, as Prime Minister and as party leader, he was still on probation. Eden was not, like Churchill, the beer and bread of England. In a nation where foreign affairs are important he had staked his place in history on his record beyond England's shores. In approaching Geneva, Eden shunned, of course, the rococo presentation of Mr. Faure. His long record in the Foreign Office taught him further to distrust the American instinct for personal contact with the Russians. The only serious program for German unification, the Eden Plan, was his own creation. So he elaborated it and set out to make it more acceptable for the Russians in a series of proposals on partial neutrality for Germany. These he listed as "examples" in deference to Mr. Dulles' distrust of the specific. "We will lay them on the table at Geneva," said one of his aides, "and watch closely to see when Russian eyes light up."

Eisenhower, in contrast, cast aside the subtleties and the complexities of the Eden proposals, sensing in his unerring way that when chiefs of state meet, only great and simple gestures are deeply felt and long remembered. In this spirit he resolved to act on his own. Earlier delegations of the Presidential powers to Admiral Radford and Secretary Dulles had on more than one occasion landed Eisenhower close to disaster. So in Geneva he determined that he would play the President's part. Lacking Roosevelt's jaunty conviction that he could charm the buttons off Stalin's vest, Eisenhower had enough of Roosevelt in him to believe that he could redirect the course of world diplomacy by the force of his personal impact on the Soviet leaders. And on the one issue of disarmament on which he trusted his own judgment, the President worked alone, without the knowledge of his own delegation.

So the final preparations were made for Geneva. In inspired editorials of the *London Times*, through quiet briefings of the American reporters, and in the spirited debate which Premier Faure staged with French journalists, the outlines of the Western position became clearer. The Russians, in turn, matched every dramatic development with one of their own. Two senior Soviet advisers on Germany were added to the Russian delegation. Then Marshal Zhukov's participation was announced in a plain bid for direct talks with Eisenhower. Next Khrushchev said that he was coming. The reason, American experts supposed, was that Khrushchev was anxious to share the credit for any success that might be registered at Geneva, while all the other Soviet leaders wanted to be quite sure that in the event of failure Khrushchev would share the blame.

So, in Paris the sense of excitement mounted, despite the warnings of old-timers that nothing could take place. "We're dealing with three mavericks in our chiefs of state," said one expert. "Who knows," he added, "the conference may amount to something after all."

From then on, of course, the outcome of the Conference turned on the Russians. If their purpose at Geneva was propaganda, they would endorse the Faure Plan and blame the United States for withholding from the masses its immediate fruits. If instead they wanted rapid progress toward a real settlement, even at some cost to themselves, then they would advance to a detailed examination of the Eden proposals. But if their main objective was to create a better international atmosphere without giving up anything of significance, then Eisenhower's appeal for a new spirit would be the one to which the Soviet leaders would respond.

It was the third course that the Russians chose at Geneva. They showed a new spirit of friendliness from the moment that they walked down the ramp of their plane. They demonstrated in particular an ardent desire to please the Americans and a touching capacity to be pleased by the Americans in return. But they did not relate the new spirit to any new plans for peace. They advanced over the five days of the conference a series of detailed proposals. But all of these proved on close examination to be repetitions of familiar propositions with only minor modifications. Bulganin and Molotov, in other words, came to Geneva with precisely the same thought as Eisenhower and Dulles: the Conference should create a new spirit, but one not sustained by any new ideas.

It was on the opening day of the Conference that the Russians scored their great success. They arrived at the Palais des Nations in an open car in obvious contrast to President Eisenhower who roared by encased in a bullet-proof limousine escorted by motorcycle policemen and surrounded by armed guards. In further contrast, the leader of the free peoples hurried unsmiling up the steps of the Palais while the heirs of Stalin paused with a wave and a smile on each step. The President spoke first in the morning and, in homage to his party, voiced his concern over the enslavement of the satellite states. In the first of many rumors started in the Maison de la Presse, French journalists reported that the Russians were upset. The polemics of the President, they felt, made it hard for them not to engage in counter-polemics, and yet they had no desire to see the Conference start on a sour note. But if the Soviet delegates felt the temptation to argue, they resisted it. Marshal Bulganin, it seemed, had chosen as his model for Geneva the prior success of his side at Bandung. There Chou En-lai had brilliantly countered rudeness with courtesy, and extremism with moderation. The Russians were determined to appear even more mature. In one mild word "inappropriate" Marshal Bulganin passed over the President's unkind phrases. "The purpose of this conference," Bulganin stated in an exact paraphrase of the President's main point, "is not to indulge in recrimination but to . . . create an atmosphere of confidence in relations between nations."

So the new spirit survived. "If we can preserve this spirit of friendship," declared the President at the close of the first day, "then . . . this conference will be a great success."

With equal determination the Soviet and American delegates generated the new spirit throughout a trying week. The Marshal demonstrated that he was truly moved. The President appealed to Marshal Bulganin to believe in his peaceful intentions. Marshal Bulganin replied that indeed he did. Mr. Dulles, who once relished his bitter encounters with Mr. Molotov, joked about their past exchanges and approached the Soviet Foreign Minister with courtesy and respect. Mr. Molotov also joked and appeared to be open to reason. "You may be right, of course," said Mr. Molotov. "No doubt I may be mistaken. . . . I quite see your point. . . ." The veterans of ten years looked at each other in total disbelief.

In the buffet luncheons and the elaborate dinners the new spirit was maintained. The President kidded Zhukov about his many colored uniforms and Bulganin about his non-military suits. The Marshal in turn kidded Eisenhower about his new-found civilian status. Even the most cynical of diplomats was impressed. The Soviet leaders had always trusted and admired Eisenhower in the same wholehearted way in which they distrusted and feared Dulles. They are, in addition, sober students of protocol who respect rank with the same intensity as they revere power. Quite apart from personality there is a majesty that surrounds a President in Soviet eyes. To this majesty Eisenhower added human warmth. He was riding a crest of self-confidence at Geneva, passionately believing in his mission and at the same time thoroughly enjoying himself. His earnestness and friendliness were pressed upon Bulganin and Khrushchev who had barely met an American, and the impression was apparently profound.

There were, however, iron boundaries where the excursion of personal diplomacy came to a halt. They were reached on the second day when German unification dominated the agenda. The Allied leaders had pressed hard for unification during the first day's discussions. Marshal Bulganin had spoken in rather vague and encouraging phrases. He agreed that German unification was the goal. He maintained only that it must be accomplished step by step, which was a position that German spokesmen themselves advanced in private conversation.

This view was not beyond reconciliation with Allied demands. For the Allies agreed in private that a period of lowered tensions would necessarily precede a solution in Germany. They feared principally that the Russians would look on this period not as an interval of relaxation but as an opportunity for active intrigue to extract West Germany from NATO. Lacking any evidence that the Soviet thaw extended beyond smiles to minds and hearts, they pressed the Soviet delegation on the second day for prompt assurances on specific points. Thus cornered, Marshal Bulganin chose to be frank. He declared that the time for unification had not come and could not be fixed.

So Eden was brushed aside. It remained for Eisenhower to try his alternative approach. The President fixed his eyes on Zhukov and declared that the Russians had nothing to fear from NATO. But an impression is less than a conversion, and conversion required a greater figure than Eisenhower at Geneva. Bulganin closed the day with finality, declaring that his statement reflected the well-considered view of the Soviet Government and that he would say no more.

On the third day the Conference turned to security. To Mr. Dulles the issue was very clear. Seen as an abstraction, he believed European security was a meaningless effort to join six or twenty-six nations in the common illusion that there was some safety in paper promises.

Seen instead as a means of limiting the dangers attendant upon German unification, a security system moved into focus as a set of well-defined and well-enforced guarantees. These guarantees would concern the frontiers, the alliances, and the armed forces of a unified Germany, and therefore, Dulles argued, security for Europe could be considered only in the context of German unification.

But unification had been set aside by Bulganin, and on security the Russians had a plan apart. A new and realistic proposal on security might have recovered for the Russians the ground lost on the previous day. But their proposal proved in all essentials to be the plan presented in Berlin eighteen months before. It did offer participation in the security system to the United States, but this concession had long been discounted. And while the plan moved toward realism in proposing two stages, the Valhalla of unification lay in the second stage and, on the farther side, of the destruction of NATO.

The United States insisted on unification before security, the Russians on security before unification. The French hinted at a plan for linking security systems, which the Germans indignantly vetoed as an unacknowledged acquiescence in the status quo. There the deadlock continued until Eden proposed that unification and security be considered together. On that basis the Foreign Ministers were sent off to work up a directive. This constructive act in turn nearly wrecked the Conference. For Eisenhower in dispatching the Ministers seemed to tell them to follow the Soviet stand. A near-panic followed in the German press, and usually responsible British journalists enlivened their nation's newsstands with preposterous stories of an American surrender to the Kremlin.

But Mr. Molotov, still gracious, saved the President from further embarrassment on the following morning by remarking that everyone understood that unification and security were linked together. That, however, appeared to be the last point on which the Foreign Ministers could agree.

The chiefs of state moved on to the great issue of disarmament. Here the Russians were on their most favorable ground. Their major proposals of May 10 stood unanswered after ten weeks, and no well-prepared answer was available on the Allied side. In his last press conference, however, and his opening address at Geneva the President had moved a substantial distance in the direction of the Soviet plan. The distance that remained in principle was not too far to prohibit a detailed directive to the UN experts to start over in the preparation of a modest and realizable program for early warning and selective inspection.

"The United States," the President declared in Thursday's session, "is prepared to enter into a sound and reliable agreement." He defined this agreement as one based on adequate inspection and reporting. "I propose," he said, "that we instruct our representatives in the subcommittee on disarmament . . . to give priority effort to the study of inspection and reporting." This was perhaps the most important recommendation of the entire conference, but it was wholly lost. The President apparently had been brooding in secret upon a much more dramatic idea, and some remark of Bulganin's prompted him to bring it forth. Setting aside his glasses and speaking "from my heart," the President proposed to exchange "immediately" the complete blueprint of our military establishments and "to provide within our countries facilities for aerial photography to the other country." The Russians said nothing. Faure regretted only that all his countrymen could not have witnessed the President's great act. Eden was a little more reserved. The French and Swiss papers called the proposal "audacious." *"Grossartig . . ."* exclaimed the admiring observers from Bonn. The American journalists, in contrast, were inclined to be resentful, feeling that they had been misled.

The President's offer certainly could scarcely have been designed to be more unacceptable to the cautious and suspicious Russians. And a good many observers, when they recovered from the first shock, concluded that the President's purpose was not to give a start to new discussions but to put an end to the Soviet boasts that his country could not match the courage and boldness of the May 10 plan. It is more charitable to accept the President's own explanation. "I have been searching in my heart and mind," he declared, "for something I could say here that could convince everyone of the great sincerity of the United States in approaching the problem of disarmament." Eisenhower presumably was still endeavoring to convert the Russians to his own belief that they had nothing to fear but fear itself and so to salvage some great achievement from the ruins of the earlier discussion on Germany. But well-meaning and daring almost to the point of recklessness as this intervention was, it seemed probable that it would do more harm than good.

The risks most certainly were very great. For the Russians are allergic to all theatrics except their own. If now they decided that the President's action was not generous impulse, but a well-prepared plan, contrived to look like an impulse, then they would be driven toward the conclusion that Ike's other acts of impulse were also contrived. And if this idea took hold in inherently suspicious minds, then the greatest of Geneva's assets—the Russian belief in Eisenhower's personal integrity—might be sacrificed on the altar of one propaganda blow.

In either event the Soviet reaction was unlikely to find expression at Geneva. For by Thursday evening the conference was moving toward its end. As the foreign ministers struggled with the final communiques, a few conclusions could be drawn.

The Soviet government came to Geneva with well-established positions. And neither the limited offers of Eden nor the personal assurances of Eisenhower could work any substantial change in these positions in the course of five days. Nor was this a cause for gloom. It was, after all, Mr. Dulles' emphatic view that a long period of study, of reflection, and of verification in subsequent meetings would be necessary before any new positions would emerge. And the Soviet leaders, as I have indicated, shared Mr. Dulles' opinion to a startling degree. Only great weakness within the Soviet Union could have led the Soviet Union to yield on Germany. And if the conference served no other purpose, it demonstrated that the Soviet state is not, as Mr. Dulles maintained, on the point of collapse.

Far from showing weakness at Geneva the Russians demonstrated that their ambitions as well as their defensive positions are unchanged. "Do not imagine," said an influential and sophisticated Russian to me, "that there has been a revolution within the Soviet Union. Mr. Khrushchev, I assure you, is following the Stalin line."

The Stalin line as last laid down at the 19th Party Congress, was that, given the right tactics by the Kremlin, wars between the capitalist countries were still as probable as capitalist war upon the Soviet world.

For the present Soviet ambitions are unaltered. And yet the new spirit is also real. It survives because both sides have need of it; the West, because free societies need hope for nourishment; the East, because the immense tasks of internal consolidation require a period of *detente,* relaxation in strained relations between nations.

The Russians insist on a period of *detente* before yielding on the great sources of tension. The West will accept the *detente* because it has no choice.

In terms of concrete agreements, the immediate gains from a relaxation are likely to be meager. But the significance of agreements can be enormously overrated today. On the great issue of disarmament, for example, we have come down to the technicalities of early warning. And yet they are far less significant than political and psychological storm signals. In Russia today, as in China last year, months of telltale psychological preparation must precede an aggressive war.

There are dangers in a *detente*. They center in Germany, where the strains of division may break apart the contracts made with the West. They can be avoided only if the Western partnership gains continually in meaning and in promise. And if the Soviet stake in the new spirit becomes so great that the penalties of a deal with Germany will seem to the Soviet leaders to outweigh its gains.

To balance this danger, there is in a *detente* one source of hope. Wise men, the experts recall here, have argued that the semi-myth of foreign hostility is indispensable in justifying the repressive instruments of the Soviet state. How far, they wonder now, can economic exploitation and police terror be maintained during a *detente?* If the relaxation should long continue, then the thaw may truly melt more than the hard resolve of the Allies.

In that event, as President Eisenhower prophesied, all problems may become manageable. NATO will shrink in significance as a military instrument. Germany will begin to look like any other state. The new spirit of Geneva will begin to take on flesh and blood. The hermits of the Kremlin will discover that there is something after all in the view that beyond their borders at least they have nothing to fear but fear itself.

JOHN LEAR

Ike and the Peaceful Atom

"ATOMS FOR PEACE" has become the one real crusade of General Dwight D. Eisenhower's period in the Presidency. The pledge he made before the surprised General Assembly of the United Nations on December 8, 1953—a solemn promise that the moment our good will was matched, we would take uranium from our A-bomb stockpile and put it in a world bank where "have-not" neighbors could borrow it for their own peaceful purposes—is still remembered and cherished in the earth's far places.

No other act of the President has commanded such universal acceptance and acclaim. And, singularly, nothing else that he has done so thoroughly typifies his own strongest personal traits: the fortitude of the soldier and the patience of the man of simple faith.

At times alone, at best with only the liberals of his party about him, always with Republican doubters and dissenters dragging out and slowing down the march, Eisenhower has slogged toward "atoms for peace" through two dismaying years, stopping often for stragglers, until now, in the twenty-fifth month of his campaign, he is at last within sight of his objective.

Who helped him, who hindered him, how he mediated between them without once invoking the Presidential power of political banishment, what led him in the first place to end the long period of doubt and hesitation that had encompassed the latter half of the Truman Administration and the first quarter of his own, and finally what caused him to appear before the U.N. to bespeak a new day for the atom-frightened world—all these together make up a case history of successful American improvisation against Communist threat and duplicity, the triumph of American initia-

"Ike and the Peaceful Atom" by John Lear (Science Editor of *Saturday Review*) is from the June 12, 1956 issue of *The Reporter*.

tive over American caution, and the growth of American idealism from the roots of American practicality.

Like the Marshall Plan before it, "atoms for peace" sprang from strategic and psychological necessity. When President Eisenhower took office, the atomic armaments race had been going on for four years. The Russians had exploded their first A-bomb in 1949, and the President knew it would be only a matter of time before they duplicated the vastly more powerful hydrogen bomb we had set off late in 1952. The urgency and tension of waiting for that bigger Soviet bomb to drop were heightened by the death of Joseph Stalin barely six weeks after Eisenhower's term opened.

Stalin had given every sign of indifference to the wholesale slaughter of atomic warfare. Would the new men in the Kremlin feel differently? And would they understand that atomic weapons had now ruled out any alternatives to peace?

Within a few weeks after Stalin's death, Eisenhower put the question directly to the new rulers in the Kremlin. Is there, he asked in a speech in April, 1953, a "chance for a just peace . . . ?"

No one in Washington expected an answer soon. Until one came, it was imperative to prepare the American people for the worst. Ever since 1950, the Pentagon had argued that the full truth about atomic holocausts should be told. It had to be made clear that we held no monopoly on atomic knowledge. President Truman had not accepted this military appraisal—at least not enough to act on it. President Eisenhower did accept it, wholeheartedly, and some time before or during the month of April, 1953, he and the National Security Council agreed to reveal to the people here at home the facts of life in the H-bomb era.

Among the many agents of this revelation, two had prominent roles. One was C. D. Jackson, who had taken a leave of absence as publisher of *Fortune* magazine to run psychological warfare at the White House. The other was Lewis L. Strauss, a Wall Street investment banker who had sat on the original Atomic Energy Commission from 1946 to 1950, and had been brought back into the government by Eisenhower, first as personal adviser to the President in atomic matters and then as AEC Chairman.

As a professional jounalist, Jackson wanted to inform the public with all possible impact. As the official guardian of atomic secrets, Strauss wanted to withhold everything that touched in the slightest degree on security. Between the two opposing points of view stood the President, encouraging both without offending either. Scores of drafts of a public declaration on the atom were written and circulated through the AEC and the Pentagon during 1953 in what later became known as Operation CANDOR.

The first batch was produced from April to June. Collectively, they have since been characterized by the single word "Bang!" because they pictured the frightful wounds an H-bomb could inflict upon the United States. In May, Jackson came up with such a realistic and grisly recital that the President shuddered and turned away, saying, "We don't want to scare the country to death!"

A second batch started circulating in July. They became known as the "Bang! BANG!" papers because they linked the horrors atomic bombs could visit upon us to the devastation we would wreak in retaliation. It was thought that the second, bigger BANG would be somewhat reassuring. But at the end of the month, after dozens of drafts had been shuffled all over Washington, the President read the finished paper, shook his head, and said, "This leaves everybody dead on both sides, with no hope anywhere. Can't we find some hope?"

Jackson, for one, had just about given up hope when the Russians exploded their first H-bomb early in August, 1953.

The President was in Denver when he got the news of the Russian explosion. He thought back to his years as Supreme Commander of SHAPE and remembered how fearful our Allies had been of our atomic intentions. He reviewed in his mind the reports that our ambassadors and ministers had been sending to the White House from neutral nations like India, whose peoples saw our atomic attitude as a new form of "imperialistic warmongering."

Perhaps, the President concluded, the time had come to test an assumption that had long tantalized him—the idea that the best chance for lasting peace was to undertake disarmament in small, cautious steps, thus allowing time to build up mutual confidence. What, he asked himself, could he propose as the first step? After turning the problem over in his mind for a while, he called a secretary and dictated a memo that read something like this:

"I have been thinking about this atom business, and it seems to me there ought to be some way for us to give a certain amount of uranium to some kind of international agency that might be set up for the purpose. We couldn't give much at first without scaring our own people. But it should be enough to show the have-not peoples of the world that we sincerely want to develop the atom in a peaceful, friendly way. What are the technical problems we would have to work out in order to do this?"

Those were not his exact words, but they express the President's meaning as closely as his press secretary, James C. Hagerty, can remember it. The memo was carried from Denver to Washington and delivered to Lewis Strauss.

Strauss had come into the Administration from the right wing of the Republican party. Once a secretary to Herbert Hoover and a close friend of Senator Taft, the AEC Chairman had been an investment banker in Wall Street and had acquired a portly suavity which, with his short stature, gave him a marked resemblance to a well-dressed owl.

Like the owl, Strauss said more with his eyes than with his mouth. In talking to me about atoms for peace, he would neither confirm nor deny that he had ever received the President's memo from Denver. He acted as though I hadn't mentioned it. The truth may be that Strauss would have preferred never to have seen the memo. His wariness concerning all atomic dealings with foreign nations was a matter of record. At a congressional investigation into alleged mismanagement of the AEC in 1949, he had stated his philosophy plainly: "My observation is that international friendships are ephemeral."

Strauss was then a member of the original AEC, named in 1946 by President Truman. He was undoubtedly the most conservative of Truman's five appointees. He opposed his four colleagues on the very first international question that came before the Commission in 1947. The issue was whether radioactive isotopes ought to be shipped to our friends abroad.

Atomic scientists had pleaded for regular shipments in return for reports on experiments that would ensue. The scientists' reasoning was that the fissioning of uranium could not be obscured from the rest of the world for very long anyway. It was important, therefore, that we should have some open channel through which to learn of new atomic discoveries.

The Atomic Energy Act of 1946 permitted isotope shipments "for research or development activity, medical therapy, industrial uses, or such other useful applications as may be developed." At the same time, the law specifically prohibited "exchange of information with other nations with respect to the use of atomic energy for industrial purposes . . . until Congress declares by joint resolution that effective and enforceable international safeguards against the use of atomic energy for destructive purposes have been established . . ."

Strauss considered isotopes themselves to be a kind of information, or at least a possible source of information. He consequently interpreted the ban on information to cover isotopes in all cases that might involve industry, directly or indirectly. "I am not an isolationist and have never been," he insisted. "National security, however, as long as I am a member of this Commission, must be my paramount responsibility."

After being voted down four to one, and declared in error by the AEC's legal counsel, Strauss asked for and obtained his associates' consent to carry a personal appeal from their verdict on isotopes to the State Department and the Pentagon. The appeals failed, but Strauss was still convinced that he was in the right in the matter.

When Strauss returned to the AEC as Chairman, neither the law nor his interpretation of it had changed one bit. So when he was told that a Communist professor in a Norwegian university laboratory had actually used an American radioisotope during the period when Strauss had been fighting isotope shipments abroad, the AEC Chairman saw an opportunity to vindicate his solitary judgment.

All discussion of the incident is taboo at the State Department today, and Strauss's hand does not appear openly anywhere. But it is generally accepted that Strauss was responsible for a violent security investigation of diplomatic channels between Oslo and Washington. The fulminations turned up evidence that the State Department had known of the Communist professor, had investigated him, and had dismissed him as a harmless, talkative old man who never actually did anything in support of the Moscow line and always conducted his isotope experiments in the open classroom with his pupils about him. The innocence or guilt of the professor was not Strauss's concern. The crucial point to him was that the professor's existence had been known and had not been reported to the AEC.

In the shake-up that followed, the ablest atomic student in the State Department, R. Gordon Arneson—one of those who had been unable to accept Strauss's interpretation of the law on isotopes—was removed as Special Assistant to the Secretary of State on Atomic Energy Affairs, and exiled to an observer's post at the Imperial Defense College in London. To Arneson's old desk came Gerard Smith of the AEC, who is said to be an amiable fellow but who shuns all contact with reporters. For practical purposes, his office has become a branch of Strauss's office, and requests for clarification of foreign policy on the atom are frankly referred back to the AEC.

Only a few weeks after this practical demonstration of the vigor of Strauss's vigilance on the foreign front, during the summer of 1953, he received the memo from President Eisenhower in Denver. The memo proposed what amounted to an international bank of atoms for peace. Of course such a bank would necessarily lend or sell uranium. Now if isotopes were dangerous "information" that should not be permitted to fall into alien hands, in what category was uranium?

Uranium is fissionable material. The Atomic Energy Act of 1946 made it quite clear that "The [Atomic Energy] Commission shall not (1) distribute any fissionable material to . . . any foreign government . . ."

Since Strauss does not admit that he ever received Eisenhower's memo, it is hardly reasonable to expect him to reveal the contents of his reply. But he did reply, and, from what Hagerty tells me, the reply must have been to this effect:

"The law is very strict about this sort of thing. I doubt if we can do much without consulting Congress. But I'll see."

Then Strauss passed on the gist of the President's message to Jackson, who would have to decide how, when, and where the atom bank would be announced if the plan proved feasible.

The Denver memo conveyed no sense of urgency. But the President soon removed any doubt about his desire for speed. On August 19, he flew east to take part in the celebration of Bernard Baruch's birthday in New York City and to register for the elections. He sent word ahead that he would expect to see Strauss and Jackson at the Waldorf. The AEC Chairman and the psychological warfare chief traveled to New York from Washington separately. They met in the anteroom of Eisenhower's suite, and breakfasted with him.

The big item Strauss remembers having on his mind that day was the secret news that the Russians had just exploded another nuclear bomb. The scientific monitoring network that Strauss had originated years earlier detected the blast, and he wanted the President's permission to announce the event. Strauss sought this endorsement in his capacity as the President's personal atomic adviser. Eisenhower's answer was "O.K."—with the implicit understanding that the announcement would be made in Strauss's other capacity as AEC Chairman. In that second role, Strauss could act only with AEC approval. He got it, but before the AEC could get out a statement for publication, the Russians announced the explosion themselves on August 20.

The big item on Jackson's mind that morning at the Waldorf was the President's atom-bank proposal. He presented a set of four specifications the bank announcement should meet:

¶ Universal reasonableness.

¶ No loss of face for anyone through reversal of previously taken positions.

¶ Initial contributions of uranium small enough to make it possible for everyone to contribute freely without fearing crippling depletion of A-bomb stockpiles.

¶ Phrasing of such a nature that people everywhere could readily see this as only a first step.

Eisenhower approved these four points before leaving the breakfast table. Strauss, of course, was in on the talk. Hagerty was there, too, and he and Jackson discussed a possible forum for the atom-bank announcement without reaching any conclusion. Before flying back to Denver, the President said, "Let's keep this thing rolling now!"

It was apparent from his demeanor that the President expected the help of Congress in changing the law that barred his path. Two days after the Baruch birthday observance in August, 1953, he received a letter that he had every reason to understand as corroboration of his confidence. The communication came from the Chairman of the Joint Committee on Atomic Energy, Representative W. Sterling Cole of New York.

The Chairman normally spoke for a majority of the Committee, and the Committee's judgments were rarely questioned by Congress. Cole's letter, therefore, read like an advance guarantee. In it, he urged construction "as quickly as possible" of an atomic furnace "turning out large amounts of useful power, and then aid [to] our allies in the construction of similar machines . . ." The letter expressed hope that Eisenhower would "seize every opportunity to assure the world that we stand ready to share the benefits of peacetime atomic energy with decent people everywhere." Cole also stated that such legislation was being drafted for introduction at the next session.

Other members of the Joint Committee on Atomic Energy have said that they knew nothing about the atoms-for-peace proposal. Not even the full membership of the AEC had been informed. Commissioner Thomas E. Murray's curiosity was aroused by a rumor, but he was told that all the President had in mind was a program to drive home to the public the facts of life in the H-bomb era—not a new atomic policy. For Washington, the degree of secrecy maintained was remarkable. Dozens of drafts of the President's proposal were in circulation from August until November, 1953. But disclosure of the atom-bank idea was averted by the publicity given Jackson's cover phrase: Operation CANDOR.

Jackson wrote somewhere between twelve and fourteen "final" drafts before he could pin the State and Defense Departments down to words they would accept, and, as someone aptly put it, "encourage Strauss to pin himself down." A great deal of what Eisenhower wanted to say was eliminated in this process. What or why, no one is willing to divulge. There is a widespread conviction in Washington that during this period Strauss did his best to kill the bank concept or at least render it innocuous. Both Jackson and Hagerty deny this, using the same cryptic phrase: "Strauss only pointed out the objections."

In any event, the atoms-for-peace bank idea survived into November, and became the hopeful alternative to "Bang! BANG!" in what Jackson called "the first honest-to-God draft" of a state paper for the President's signature. All Strauss's objections had at last been met or outvoted. It was now high time to decide when and where that state paper would be delivered.

From the very beginning the President had thought in terms of a domestic audience. The world would be looking over his shoulder, of course. The atoms-for-peace bank probably would have been suggested in a Republican equivalent of an F.D.R. "fireside chat" if it had not been for Winston Churchill.

As Britain's Prime Minister, Churchill that spring had urged a Big Four meeting "at the summit" to feel out the intentions of Stalin's successors. The United States was absolutely opposed to such a conference at that time. But we could not simply say "No" to Churchill. In a typical compromise, Eisenhower suggested that instead of meeting the Russians, he and Churchill should meet each other and the French Premier at Bermuda.

Set first for June, the Bermuda conference was postponed, because of a French Cabinet crisis, to July; and again, because of the stroke Churchill suffered that summer, to December. The latter delay turned out to be good timing for the President's purposes. The final meeting date preceded by only a few days the closing session of the U.N. General Assembly. Careful maneuvering would make it possible to meet Churchill, politely turn aside his "summit" plan, tell him about the atoms-for-peace bank, and then come back to New York and formally suggest the atom bank to the U.N. Assembly.

The tactic was quickly put into motion. Ike had received a standing invitation to the U.N. at the time of his inauguration. On the eve of Bermuda, the permanent United States representative at the U.N., Henry Cabot Lodge, Jr., was instructed to advise U.N. Secretary General Dag Hammarskjold that the President would be pleased to honor a specific renewal of the standing welcome. At the same time, Churchill was informed that Eisenhower would like to include atomic matters on the agenda for Bermuda.

The President took off for Bermuda with Dulles, Strauss, Jackson, and Hagerty—the U.N. invitation not yet confirmed. They took copies of the atom-bank message with them. At Bermuda the White House party found, as it had hoped, that the British Prime Minister was accompanied by his atomic adviser, Lord Cherwell.

The President did not intrude his big idea into the formal gatherings of the Bermuda delegations. But on the first day, after Lodge telephoned from New York to confirm Hammarskjold's invitation, the President told Churchill about it in private and authorized informal conversations among others who were present.

The French shrugged their shoulders. Whatever the President wanted to say was all right with them. Churchill felt differently. The tone of the draft he read was too belligerent. It put too much stress on the horrors of H-bomb retaliation. It might heighten Allied fears of preventive war. It definitely would jeopardize any hopeful approach to "the summit."

To allay Churchill's qualms, the draft was referred to Cherwell and Strauss. Out of several meetings of the two atomic experts emerged an agreement in principle that Cherwell persuaded Churchill "not to oppose." Exactly what was involved probably will not be known until Strauss writes his memoirs. One source says, "Strauss made the atom bank possible right there." That, certainly, is an overstatement. Eisenhower had no intention of permitting the British or anyone else to dictate significant changes in a speech to be delivered by an American President. Strauss himself says he is unable to recall talking to Cherwell about anything other than the possibility of a world conclave of scientists interested in atoms for peace.

The gratuitous emphasis that Strauss—a banker by profession—threw on atomic science at just the moment when everyone else was thinking about atomic banking would seem to indicate how the AEC Chairman really felt. It was not a simple matter of the law's prohibiting a bank; it was Strauss's philosophical concurrence with the law.

Even in discussing science in those days, Strauss dealt only in broad and general terms, stopping short of technology. In 1953 he was still following the line laid down in 1945 by the Manhattan District to govern declassification of atomic information: basic science first, technology later.

What almost everyone else but Strauss wanted in 1953 was technology—the finished article, atomic furnaces that could produce power immediately. The British not only recognized the universal demand but saw a tremendous commercial market in it. Cherwell's personal reaction is plain from a letter the Englishman wrote after a quite different scientific atoms-for-peace conference was held in Geneva last August. Recalling that at Bermuda he hadn't expected Strauss's original conference idea to contribute much to a breakthrough toward peace, Cherwell added, "I don't think you [Strauss] did, either."

The sudden, inconclusive end of the Bermuda talks in December, 1953, is reported to have left Churchill weeping in frustration. When newsmen left the island by plane their thoughts were far from "the summit." All were speculating on President Eisenhower's purpose in flying so dramatically back to address the United Nations that same afternoon.

Before the President's plane, the *Columbine,* took off for New York, Dulles cabled a code message to U.S. Ambassador Charles E. Bohlen in Moscow. At least a month earlier, it had been agreed that Bohlen was to get a full copy of the atom message for advance presentation to the Kremlin. As Lodge explained later to the United Nations, "The President wished to take every precaution in order to ensure that the Soviet Union government would take this proposal at its serious, sincere, long-term, face value, and not interpret it as a short-term propaganda trick."

Now that the time had come, the full copy of the message was not available. Final revisions were yet to be made. But the Dulles cable told Bohlen to advise Moscow to listen to the President's words and accept them as a major policy pronouncement.

With only four hours left before Eisenhower was due to appear before the U.N. Assembly, no one was certain how much work remained to be done on the message he had to deliver immediately upon his arrival. Foolproof preparations had to be made. The responsibility fell on Hagerty.

Fortunately, in setting up the Bermuda press facilities months before, Hagerty had included a hand-operated Mimeograph. Before the flight north began on December 8, this machine was hoisted into the back corner of the President's compartment on the *Columbine*. Just forward of the President's compartment three secretaries were packed in with two electric typewriters. One of the typewriters was to cut Mimeograph stencils. The other was "jumbo," a large type face the President finds easy to read when making a speech.

Between the typewriters and the Mimeograph, at the front of the President's compartment, were two tables surrounded by swivel chairs. At one of these sat the President with Dulles, Strauss, and Jackson, all working furiously on the last draft of the manuscript. Jackson wrote, Dulles edited, Strauss objected, Eisenhower chose the word that sounded the best to him. Page by page, the copy passed to Hagerty. And Hagerty, after reading the insertions and deletions from a newspaperman's point of view, passed the copy page by page to Marie McCrum, who took it forward to Mary Jane McCaffery at the stencil-cutting typewriter.

As Mary finished typing a page, she passed it across the aisle to Ann Whitman at the jumbo typewriter. While Hagerty walked back to the President's table for the next page, Marie copyread the stencil of the last page and handed it to Army Staff Sergeant Joseph Giordano, who was busily cranking the duplicating machine.

The finished document filled nine stencils. Giordano ran off five hundred copies of each of them during the three-and-a-half-hour flight. There wasn't a quiet spot on that plane all the way from Bermuda to New York. Hagerty, going in one direction, would pass the Secret Service guards going the other way, lugging the copies from the whirling duplicator to the *Columbine*'s front compartment behind the pilot's cabin, there to be stacked in proper order on two long tables.

The *Columbine* arrived over New York with the assembly line inside it still running full tilt. The pilot had to circle for fifteen minutes and then taxi slowly on the runway after he landed so that the job could be finished. Even as the plane was rolling to a stop, the President underlined on his jumbo copy the words he wanted to emphasize. As he jabbed his pencil here and there, the Secretary of State, the Chairman of the Atomic Energy Commission, and two Special Assistants to the President collated and stapled together 350 nine-page sets of the Mimeographed copies for distribution to the press at the airport. The ink was still wet on the paper when the 150 remaining copies, not yet collated or stapled, were bundled with the wet stencils into a waiting limousine—summoned from aloft by Hagerty on the *Columbine*'s telephone—to be raced over back streets into Manhattan while the President followed a motorcycle escort along the parkways, sirens screaming.

Reporters at the U.N. got the text just ten minutes before the President rose to speak. They still had plenty of time to catch up with the story, which did not really become clear until the final third of the address.

The first two-thirds of the message were devoted to the original purpose of Operation CANDOR, "thoughts I had originally planned to say primarily to the American people." Atomic bombs were twenty-five times as powerful now as in 1945; hydrogen bombs exploded with a force equivalent to millions of tons of TNT; one air group could deliver destruction equal to that of all the bombs dropped on Britain during World War II, atomic weapons now came in enough variety and sizes to be considered conventional. It was made clear that no one nation had an atomic monopoly any more: "even a vast superiority in numbers of weapons, and a consequent capability of devastating retaliation, is no preventive, of itself, against the fearful material damage and toll of human lives that would be inflicted by surprise aggression . . ."

The President almost backed into his revolutionary proposal, so slow and deliberate was his approach. ". . . to help us move out of the dark chamber of horrors into the light," he cautioned, "we must not lack patience. . . . many steps will have to be taken over many months before the world can look at itself one day and truly realize that a new climate of mutually peaceful confidence is abroad. . . ."

But "the gravity of the time is such that every new avenue of peace, no matter how dimly discernible, should be explored. . . . There is . . . one new avenue . . . not yet explored." Reference was made to a resolution suggested by the U.N. Disarmament Commission only in the previous month of November, calling for private talks of the powers "principally involved." "The United States . . . is instantly prepared to meet. . . . to hasten the day when fear of the atom will begin to disappear from the minds of people . . .

"I therefore make the following proposals:

"The governments principally involved, to the extent permitted by elementary prudence, to begin now and continue to make joint contributions from their stockpiles of normal uranium and fissionable materials to an international atomic energy agency. We would expect that such an agency would be set up under the aegis of the United Nations."

This was clearly not the announcement of a *fait accompli.* It was merely a suggestion. Details were left to be determined in "the private conversations." Eisenhower promised nothing but "explorations in good faith." He emphasized "undoubtedly" that "initial and early contributions . . . would be small in quantity," that the Soviet Union must, of course, be one of the governments "principally involved," and that "every expectation of approval" was all the President of the United States could offer on his own authority—naturally he would have to "submit [the proposal] to the Congress of the United States."

But the long string of careful qualifications vanished from the delegates' minds when they heard the President's bold declaration that "peaceful power from atomic energy is no dream of the future [but] . . . is here—now—today." The "ifs" and "buts" were forgotten in the organ swell of lofty purposes behind the President's proposed atoms-for-peace agency:

". . . to devise methods whereby this fissionable material would be allocated to . . . peaceful pursuits . . .

". . . to provide abundant electrical energy in the power-starved areas of the world . . .

". . . to serve the needs rather than the fears of mankind."

Already the effect was electric, but the President soared on to a thrilling finale:

"The United States pledges before you—and therefore before the world—its determination . . . to devote its entire heart and mind to find the way by which the miraculous inventiveness of man shall not be dedicated to his death, but consecrated to his life."

There were tears in the President's eyes when he sat down. Even the Russian delegates so far forgot themselves as to join in the thunder of applause.

U.S. Delegate Henry Cabot Lodge drove the President to the airport after the ceremonies were over. When he got home later that evening, he was astonished to receive a telephone call from a man who had never been notably friendly. Krishna Menon, India's U.N. delegate, wanted to come over to Lodge's apartment for a talk. Lodge tried to excuse himself, saying that it was late and he was very tired. Menon persisted. Lodge finally agreed. The Indian came and went on enthusiastically about Eisenhower's proposal for several hours, leaving his unwilling host not only completely exhausted but somewhat confused.

Hadn't Menon heard the whole speech? Had he missed the President's reference to Congress, which had to approve the proposal? Was he overlooking Eisenhower's proviso that the Russians had to join up before any atoms could be put into the bank?

That next week, in Washington, Strauss was similarly nonplused by an encounter with Canadian Ambassador Arnold D. Heeney. Around the globe, heads of U.S. missions were also queried by other governments, and they in turn queried the regional desks in the State Department: "What are we going to do about this?"

A long and puzzling silence followed. In February, 1954, the President—responding to political pressure from Republican businessmen who hoped to share in private development of the peaceful atom—submitted to Congress proposals for amending the Atomic Energy Act. He limited himself to the purposes endorsed the year before by the National Security Council: encouragement of private industry and help to our Allies. He specifically asked that "consideration of additional legislation which may be needed to implement . . . that proposal [to the General Assembly of the United Nations last December] . . . should await the development of areas of agreement . . . with other nations."

The impression grew, as time passed and the silence lengthened, that Eisenhower, tricked by his advisers into making a propaganda speech, had been caught flat-footed by the clamorous response of a hopeful world. A private organization was even proposed to carry out the President's idea if the government couldn't follow through with it. By April, Strauss felt impelled to acknowledge publicly "an impression . . . that nothing is going on and that the [atom-bank] proposal is dormant.

"This," he declared, "is not the case. The President's idea has been formulated into a concrete plan. . . . private conversations have ensued."

Not until September, 1954, when the U.N. was again in session, did the people find out about what had happened:

The President had begun by accepting realistically the fact that the atom bank as he had conceived it—an institution that would progressively draw uranium away from armaments everywhere and put the explosive material to peaceful uses—could only exist with Russian cooperation. So he not only insisted on including the Soviets in the discussions: he actually restricted the opening talks to them alone. How far he had gone was later revealed at the U.N. by Lodge:

"After the speech was made, and awaiting an initiative from the Soviet Union to hold private conversations, all individuals and agencies of the United States government were instructed to remain silent as to the details of the proposal and to confine themselves, if the need for explanation arose, to a simple reiteration of the President's own text and the statement that we were awaiting word from the Soviet Union."

The Russians had good reason to welcome the delay caused by Eisenhower's courtesy. Within six months they would be ready to announce the beginning of full-time operation of the world's first atomic furnace exclusively devoted to generation of peaceful atomic power. That physical reality, they calculated, would be far stronger propaganda in the power-starved regions of the world than any amount of talk about peaceful atoms. Moscow accordingly dragged out the conversations by resorting to long periods of silence interspersed occasionally with sudden bursts of double talk.

In March, 1954, the President tried to end the haggling by offering a detailed American plan for an atom bank, with an autonomous directorate reporting to the U.N. General Assembly and the Security Council. The bank would maintain its own facilities for storing and distributing uranium, disseminate information, enforce health and safety regulations, and operate its own laboratories, technical schools, and plants for the fabrication and processing of atomic fuel.

This plan the Russian rejected as a "further intensification" of the arms race, arguing that any atomic furnace capable of producing power could also produce the raw material used in bombs. "It is not enough to divert uranium from future A-bombs," the Kremlin argument ran. "You first must scrap all the A-bombs you have now."

While the Communists maneuvered to avoid the honest understanding sought by the President, the isolationist bloc of the Republican party in Congress did its bit to nullify any agreement that Eisenhower might succeed in reaching.

Instead of postponing action until a specific atom-bank agreement was ready for approval, as the White House message of February had requested, Republican Senators John Bricker of

Ohio and Bourke Hickenlooper of Iowa, partisans of Strauss in his battle against isotope exports years before, injected their personal prejudices into the new Atomic Energy Act. As members of the joint Committee on Atomic Energy, they were able to swing that strategic group away from the sympathy Representative Cole had expressed toward the President's objective in his letter of August 21, 1953.

"We can all agree, I think, as to the general desirability of an international atomic-energy pool in a world at peace," Bricker declaimed on the Senate floor. "Personally, however, I have grave doubts that it is possible to create such a pool in the present international climate without endangering the security of the United States. . . . In my judgment, it would be the height of folly for the Congress to authorize the President to transfer special nuclear material and secret atomic-energy information to the United Nations, or to any of its specialized agencies, or to any group of nations."

". . . We limit it [congressional approval] to bilateral agreements with one nation . . . ," Hickenlooper added, and Bricker agreed: "I do see the need for making agreements for cooperation with Great Britain, with Canada, and several other countries that have in the past made significant contributions to our atomic-energy program."

Eisenhower's predecessors in the Presidency had successfully fought invasions of Executive prerogative such as were written into the Atomic Energy Act of 1954. The new law, drafted in recognition of the peaceful atom's emergence as a force in world politics, anachronistically required that any atomic agreement negotiated with another country must lie before a sitting Congress for thirty days before taking legal effect. "I urged the President to accept it," Strauss has said.

"The trimmers have been at work," stormed Senator John Pastore (D., Rhode Island), in a losing fight to give the President a free hand in the atomic negotiations. "The fear-mongers have taken over. . . . Too many can see only the things that might go wrong . . . we are afraid of our own strength.

"And where have the spokesmen and advisers of American foreign policy been all these months? What have they done to keep this idea alive? The Voice of America gave . . . a big buildup at first, but . . . the idea is now mentioned always in the past tense. Its ultimate death seems to be as much aided by Americans as it is sought and worked for by the Kremlin."

Pastore was right. The President's atom-bank idea was almost dead when it reached the 1954 U.N. Assembly. The President did his best to save it by announcing, on Labor Day, 1954, that he would go ahead without the Russians if necessary. That was two months after the Soviets had started generating the world's first round-the-clock flow of electric power from an atomic furnace not otherwise devoted to any military purpose. When Moscow heard of Eisenhower's decision, it promptly did an about-face. Maybe an atom bank wasn't entirely unacceptable after all. Would the United States agree to publish the diplomatic notes that had been exchanged on the question since January?

Publication of these documents exposed, as the Kremlin intended it should, the retreat the Republicans had made from the President's original generosity. In place of the autonomous, businesslike bank that Washington had offered to support in March, what was now being proposed, as the British described it, was more like a brokerage house, with no operating facilities, empowered only to arrange and approve direct bilateral dealings between the world's uranium "haves" and "have-nots."

To present some semblance of action in fulfillment of the ideals the President had expressed a year earlier, the State Department reported to the U.N. that a charter for the atomic brokerage house was being drawn up with the help of the other "haves"—Britain, France, Canada, Belgium, South Africa, Australia, and Portugal. After the charter was ratified, Secretary Dulles explained, its framers would recommend an appropriate relationship between the atomic institution and the U.N.

The U.N. delegates who heard this report were still fired by the hope Eisenhower had raised in 1953, still enthusiastic enough to fight to keep it alive. Sweden questioned "whether it is advisable to present this agency to us as an accomplished fact . . . with the question of its link with the United Nations being left for a future stage." Yugoslavia felt "it would be appropriate to enable the member states of the United Nations which are not now participating in the present phase of the talks to make a constructive contribution . . ."

Pakistan expressed "anxiety that representation should be provided for the underdeveloped countries." Israel urged "a role for the United Nations itself, beyond the limits of research and scientific interchange." Norway called for "a radically new and more adequate arrangement" to match the total newness of the Atomic Age.

"I am afraid that a modest program will not be able to sustain the universal enthusiasm and optimism that President Eisenhower's proposal has justly aroused," the Nationalist Chinese delegate chided. Liberia hoped "that we shall not continue to be the orphan child to be fed the crumbs from the table."

Finally there rose a man whose country owes its independence to the liberality of the American spirit, Carlos Romulo of the Philippines. "It may very well be that domestic laws require some nations to carry on atomic co-operation on a bilateral basis at this moment," he said. "But laws can be changed. . . .

"I believe that we should launch the United Nations on its own co-operative atomic . . . project, inviting . . . every country able to provide even a token contribution. . . .

"The Soviet Union and the United States, which have been setting off so many atomic weapons, should be willing to contribute . . . say, 220 pounds of fissionable material, which was the maximum size the first scientific report of the United Nations Atomic Energy Commission estimated as possibly needed for a single bomb."

Romulo's challenge rang particularly shrill in the ears of one of his hearers. C. D. Jackson, who had spent months writing inspired phrases for the Eisenhower message of a year before, had left the White House staff in April a frustrated man and was now being further frustrated as a U.N. delegate.

"Give us some uranium," Jackson pleaded to Washington. "Give us some stuff that we can put out here on the table."

But Washington was silent.

At three o'clock on the afternoon of November 15, 1954, the American delegation had its last chance to save the President's great dream. Lodge was already in his chair, and the Norwegian scheduled to precede him on the floor was beginning to speak when the telephone rang in the Delegates' Lounge.

The call was for Jackson. Washington was on the line. If the message was what Jackson hoped for, it couldn't be taken there within public earshot. He raced upstairs to Lodge's private office. Strauss's voice came on the phone and said cryptically, "You've got it!"

Jackson grabbed a pencil and a piece of paper. Feverishly he wrote two paragraphs and read them to Strauss. Strauss proposed some changes. Jackson made the revisions and read the two paragraphs again. Strauss approved and hung up.

Downstairs, the Norwegian was concluding his remarks when Jackson burst into the committee room. Out of breath, the publisher leaned down to whisper in Lodge's ear and slip the paper with the news from Strauss under the last page of Lodge's notes. Lodge nodded and got up to speak. At the end of his argument, he picked up the paper and read:

"I have just been authorized by the President of the United States to state to this committee that the Atomic Energy Commission has allocated one hundred kilograms of fissionable material . . ."

One hundred kilograms was 220 pounds, the very amount Romulo had asked for as a beginning.

A man sitting within three feet of Russia's Andrei Vishinsky was fascinated by the Russian's reaction. "All through Lodge's speech," this observer recalls, "Vishinsky had been, as usual, scribbling notes for his rebuttal. When Lodge unexpectedly mentioned the hundred kilograms of uranium, there was absolute silence in the hall. Vishinsky looked up, shrugged his shoulders, reached for his briefcase, threw in his notes, put the briefcase down, and sat back in his chair. He had had it."

Vishinsky need not have been so discouraged. The hundred kilograms of uranium had not been allocated to the atoms-for-peace agency. It was designated for research only, and was to be disbursed under strictly bilateral agreements. There was still no fuel for the atomic power that Eisenhower had promised was "here —now."

Only an optimist could have believed, as Senator Pastore proclaimed, that "despite all the chipping away . . . that has been done . . . by both the Kremlin and the ill-advised counselors here at home, that [great] idea still stands."

Once again, however, Senator Pastore proved right. Eisenhower, refusing to be defeated, enlisted two new recruits—Morehead Patterson and Nelson Rockefeller—in the atoms-for-peace crusade. "Get this thing off dead center," he charged them, "and keep it off!"

Patterson, a shrewd New York industrialist who had served as Deputy U.S. Representative on the U.N. Disarmament Commission, acquired a new title: U.S. Representative for International Atomic Energy Negotiations. A husky, confident extrovert, he began the job by facing the facts, an attitude that was in itself a novelty.

"There is no possible way to prevent peaceful atoms from being perverted to warlike purposes if someone wants war badly enough," he told his aides. "But if we are going to live in the atomic age, we have to take the risks that are normal to that age.

"Someone who has atoms must give the first atom. If we don't do it, somebody else will. We may as well take the risk of being first in order to escape the danger of being last."

The statute for the atomic brokerage house, Patterson decided, could stand against the battering of the years only if it were as broad and all-inclusive as the charter of a Delaware corporation. He worked on this document exclusively from the day of his appointment in November, 1954, until March, 1955. "In March," he says, "I suddenly woke up."

What he woke up to was the fact that world faith in Eisenhower's good intentions was again being allowed to die of inattention. Everything else had been put to one side awaiting organization of the brokerage house, which would be months in process. Not even the narrow bilateral negotiations permitted by the Republican isolationists were being pushed. Congress would adjourn in June. Since under the law all atomic agreements had to lie before a Congress then in session for thirty days before taking legal effect, someone had to act fast if the whole program were not to be put off for still another long period.

Patterson called the situation to the attention of Gerard Smith, the AEC man Strauss had put into the State Department to replace Gordon Arneson. Smith threw up his hands. His meager staff was made up of AEC men with no diplomatic experience and diplomats with no knowledge of the atom. Would Patterson be so kind as to do the negotiating?

Patterson would, and did—at record-smashing speed. The method he worked out with an AEC lawyer was almost childish in its simplicity: a treaty drawn like a form letter, with blank spaces to be filled in here and there. Twenty-four copies of it were signed by as many countries in three months.

Strauss resented Patterson's activity. He said the Special Ambassador had no business intervening in the bilateral negotiations. Over on Capitol Hill, however, the Joint Committee on Atomic Energy was having some second thoughts about the limitations Congress had placed on the President's atomic bargaining power. "Pretty soon even Bricker won't believe in the Bricker amendment," one committeeman said by way of suggesting the extent of the shift in attitude. Summoning Patterson before it, the powerful legislative group showered him with praise.

President Eisenhower apparently shared the Joint Committee's preference for Patterson's free-swinging approach. At any rate, Nelson Rockefeller, the second man chosen to expedite the atoms-for-peace program in 1954, had that same cast of mind and temperament.

Rockefeller moved over from a post as Under Secretary of Health, Education, and Welfare to fill Jackson's vacant place at the White House. Having knocked around in the government under both Democratic and Republican Presidents, he had more practice than his predecessor in avoiding the petty political traps inside great issues. Taking his time and checking all disputable points carefully, old John D.'s grandson did not resume the push toward the President's objective until June, 1955. But when the push began, it moved on all fronts simultaneously.

Immediate and practical meaning was given to the bilateral agreements Patterson had negotiated. All friendly nations whose atomic technology was weak were offered not only uranium for research (and the hundred kilograms announced for that purpose at the U.N. was doubled) but also half the cost of research atomic furnaces in which to use the fuel.

Regional research and training centers as well as research furnaces were offered to countries with special power problems, such as the members of the Columbo Plan in Asia.

Countries able and willing to pay for their own atomic power were offered full opportunity to buy furnaces and technical advice, including classified information where necessary.

By this time, the Eisenhower spirit dominated the Washington scene so unmistakably that it swept up Strauss before he knew what was happening.

It will be remembered that at the Bermuda conference in December, 1953, the AEC Chairman had talked to Lord Cherwell about a world conference of atomic scientists. Why Strauss wanted the kind of meeting he did has never been explained. Similar conferences already had been held in Europe, and had exhausted the significant data in all but one field: atomic power. Strauss was opposed to any open discussion of power. That left nothing new for the scientists to talk about and nothing to be done beyond pompous posturing.

At first Strauss planned to hold this distinguished congress in Washington, where he personally could sit on the lid of confidential data. To prevent the insinuation of political questions at any level, he thought in terms of private sponsorship, and went as far as to ask the Ford Foundation if it would pick up the check.

The Foundation declined to front for the project. Then Strauss discovered that the McCarran Immigration Act would not permit entry into this country of many Communist scientists who would necessarily have to be among the guests at any truly international gathering. So it would have to be held somewhere else. One of the purposes of his discussion with Lord Cherwell at Bermuda was to obtain British consent to hold the meeting on an island fairly near the United States, preferably Jamaica.

Not because he had changed his 1949 opinion about the elusiveness of international relationships but rather because he could not accomplish his purpose within the confines of the United States, Strauss finally asked the 1954 U.N. General Assembly to issue invitations for a science conference at Geneva in August, 1955.

The U.N. issued the invitations out of respect for the President, hoping that something would happen to dissipate Strauss's insistence on avoiding any talk about atomic power.

As Eisenhower's atomic adviser, Strauss might be able to command the attendance of American scientists. But unless power were on the agenda, the U.N. Secretariat knew, prospects of commanding the time of important foreign researchers were exceedingly dim.

Strauss, however, was not open to argument. To fortify himself, he committed the British also to oppose atomic-power talk at Geneva. The conference looked hopeless at the time the British concurrence in Strauss's view was transmitted through the Foreign Office. But diplomats who handled the matter were not aware that during their negotiations, the European Atomic Energy Society was presenting a letter to the U.N. expressing a vigorously opposing view. The letter was signed by the president of the Society, Sir John Cockcroft, the head of Britain's atomic-energy agency.

Faces turned purple when the Foreign Office learned what Sir John had done. After composure was restored, however, there was common agreement that Cockcroft's opinion had to prevail. The British government simply could not be in the position of contradicting its own No. 1 atomic expert.

The turnabout faced Strauss with the ostensible choice of allowing atomic power to be discussed or of abandoning the conference. Actually, there was no choice. The conference had been Strauss's idea—all his—and abandonment of it would be unthinkable.

Once on the agenda, atomic power took over. So much information had been dammed up on that topic for ten years that the resulting flood turned Geneva into the greatest scientific irrigation project of modern times. Before it was finished, both the Russians and the Americans were adding new data to their papers right up to the moment of delivery and even afterward.

Instead of the hostility Strauss had feared, the competition generated a friendliness that had been unknown between East and West since wartime days. At one point, an American defended the integrity of Soviet research; at another, a Russian chemist pleaded for more recognition for chemists—all chemists in all countries—as opposed to physicists, all physicists everywhere in the world.

"I wonder whether Lewis would have started it if he could have foreseen how it would end," a man close to Strauss mused afterward. "If he had known that we would come out of it holding hands with the Russians, I think he would have been aghast!"

However the AEC Chairman may have felt about it, he left Geneva an international figure. It was his conference, no matter how far it diverged from his original ideas, and he stayed with it even after it was no longer recognizable to him. Lewis Strauss came home a changed man.

"Lewis had not always done everything he could for atoms for peace," a high government official reported after Geneva. "But he's with us now all the way."

Anyone who tries to talk to Strauss about export of isotopes today is whisked away from the subject with a pleasant "Oh, that's ancient history." In an almost absent-minded way, he refers in passing to the outstandingly famous episode of his pre-Geneva life: his triumphant battle, in company with Gordon Dean, for the H-bomb. The rest of his conversation is occupied with peace. One of his aides expressed what a listener to Strauss's conversation is bound to feel: "Strauss passionately desires to be remembered as a peaceful man."

The past is not entirely forgiven. One person wholeheartedly devoted to a truly international atom told me, "When I see Strauss parading as the great advocate of atoms for peace, I am reminded of the small boy who is carried to the bathtub screaming and then comes out boasting how clean he is."

When the U.N. delegates gathered for the General Assembly in 1955, the mark of Geneva was upon them. The charter that Patterson had drafted for the atomic brokerage house was examined in a new light. From the Geneva discussions it was clear that atomic power alone was no panacea for the ills of underdeveloped nations. Atomic power can be a tremendous boon, but it can be used only as part of a broad plan of industrial and agricultural development. Many years must be spent in effecting it.

The first great market for atomic power, then, is not the poorer lands but Britain and western Europe, where power from older fuels is already falling short of existing needs. Many of the nations which make up that market prefer to take the technical data made available at Geneva and deal directly with the United States or whoever else will supply them with atomic fuel. Why should they risk involvement with a board of directors who might have competitive reasons of their own for holding up this or that atomic project?

In the long U.N. debates of 1955, the smaller powers—the underdeveloped ones that must plan development far in advance—spoke up again for an atom bank like the one Eisenhower first proposed. They wanted this institution tied closely to the U.N. from the start so that they might not later become the victims of a new form of colonialism, a form in which we would give them uranium for power only with a bilateral commitment to give us back the plutonium, a by-product, to make bombs for us.

Thanks largely to President Eisenhower's continuing initiative, expressed, in the finest American tradition, through Democratic Senator Pastore, the legitimate aspirations of the "have-nots" were finally recognized. The United States, represented in the debate by delegate Pastore, agreed to submit the charter of the atomic brokerage house to a special convention of U.N. members.

As preparations proceed for that historic meeting in 1956, there are indications that the U.S. draft of a charter may, after all, provide for a true atom bank with practical working facilities of its own. There are signs, too, given to NATO by Secretary of State Dulles on his latest trip to Europe, that the President will ask Congress for specific approval for sharing information that could make the peaceful atom an even more decisive force than he had originally contemplated—the binding element of a united Europe.

If any or all of this is to come about, someone is going to have to see to it that, in the President's own words, the program gets off dead center and stays off.

The two atomic expediters who served him best—Morehead Patterson and Nelson Rockefeller—have left the government.

Will Lewis Strauss pick up the challenge?

Or will Eisenhower remain merely within sight of the objective of what has been his greatest crusade as President?

ROBERT J. DONOVAN

Heart Attack

Mrs. Eisenhower Awakens the President—He Is Seized by a Pain in His Chest—Dr. Snyder Makes a Diagnosis and Passes a Lonely Vigil with the President—Eisenhower Is Taken to the Hospital—Nixon's Busy Night—How the Government Ran—The Cabinet Discusses Procedures for Carrying On in the President's Absence—Convalescence.

I

SHORTLY AFTER 2:30 on the morning of September 24, Mrs. Eisenhower, whose bedroom was across the hall from the President's on the second floor, heard her husband tossing about in bed. She went into his quarters to see what was disturbing him. The plain, comfortable room was familiar. On her left as she entered was a round table with a lamp. On one side of the table was a small straight chair and on the other a large overstuffed upholstered chair and ottoman. In the far wall opposite the door was a fireplace flanked by windows. To Mrs. Eisenhower's immediate right stood a shoulder-high chest of drawers and just beyond, parallel to the windows looking out on the elm-shaded street, was the large old-fashioned double bed her husband slept in. At the foot of it, completing the furnishings, was a low dresser.

Mrs. Eisenhower stepped over and found the President asleep, but because he was very restless, she woke him up.

"What's the matter, Ike?" she asked. "Are you having a nightmare or something?"

Rousing himself, the President replied that he was feeling all right, and with this assurance Mrs. Eisenhower returned to her room. The President did not drop right back to sleep, however, and within a very short time he was assailed by a pain in his chest of a kind he had never experienced before. He went into Mrs. Ei-

"Heart Attack" is from *Eisenhower: The Inside Story* by Robert J. Donovan (pp. 362-386).

senhower's room and put his hand on his chest to show where he was suffering. On the assumption that it might be a recurrence of the indigestion of the afternoon before, she gave him a dose of milk of magnesia and sent him back to bed. But not satisfied that this was sufficient, she telephoned General Snyder, who was living at the bachelor officers' quarters at Lowry four miles away.

"Ike has a pain in his chest," she said, as her words have since been recalled. "You'd better come over."

Snyder called the air-base dispatcher for a car and instructed him also to pick up a medical kit in his office on the second floor of the administration building. Without wasting a minute, the handsome, seventy-four-year-old physician, who had been Eisenhower's doctor for ten years, slipped on his clothes over his pajamas and was waiting on the steps with his bag when the car arrived, driven by Airman 2/c Jacob Judis.

"Seven hundred fifty Lafayette Street and step on it," Snyder said.

Speeding through the overcast night without paying attention to traffic lights, Judis wheeled Snyder up to the Doud house at 3:11 A.M., and the general went at once to the President's room. Eisenhower was lying in bed restless, tormented by the severe pain in his chest. He was perspiring and flushed, though the flush was slowly giving way to pallor.

Snyder listened to Eisenhower's chest with a stethoscope and took his pulse and tested his blood pressure with a band on his arm. The pressure had gone up and the pulse was rapid. It took only two or three minutes for Snyder to come to the grave conclusion that the President of the United States was suffering from a coronary thrombosis. The extent of damage to the heart he could not, of course, determine immediately.

Quickly Snyder broke an ampoule of amyl nitrate and told the President to sniff it. Following this he gave him an injection of papaverine hydrochloride to dilate the arteries in the heart and then a shot of morphine to ease the pain and shock. A little later he prepared a hypodermic of heparin, which tends to increase the liquidity of the blood and to prevent clotting, and injected it in his arm.

A tall, straight, gray-haired, bespectacled man with unbounded affection for Eisenhower, Snyder stood tensely by the bedside observing his patient. He did not tell him what his diagnosis was, but the President knew he was very ill. His pain continued. About 3:45 A.M. Snyder gave him a second shot of morphine. As it pried loose the grip of pain, the President began sliding into a deep sleep. This was a profound relief to Snyder. The President was passing through a crisis, and the physician believed that sleep was the best thing for him.

To avert shock to Mrs. Eisenhower, who has long suffered from valvular heart disease herself, Snyder sent her back to bed without telling her the President's true condition. Also, he put aside the idea of a public announcement because he feared that it would cause great excitement which inevitably would permeate the Doud house and might possibly kill the President. Sitting alone in the dead of night with his slumbering patient, therefore, Howard Snyder was the only man in the world who knew that the President was stricken with a damaged heart.

All night long and through the morning, Snyder remained in the room with the President. He left the band on Eisenhower's arm to keep check of the blood pressure. Gradually the pressure came down and his pulse slowed to a steady beat. Although the President's condition was precarious and the future inscrutable, these encouraging signs were the faint beginnings of a remarkable recovery.

Shortly before 7 A.M. when the Presidential staff began stirring at Lowry, Snyder called Mrs. Whitman, the President's secretary, and informed her that the President was not feeling well and would not come to his office for appointments. Still holding back the truth about Eisenhower's condition, he told her that he was suffering from digestive upset. Soon afterward Murray Snyder (no kin to the general) got him on the phone and the doctor repeated this description of the illness. At 10:30 A.M. Murray Snyder, whose handling of the story in the next twelve hours won the deep admiration of the reporters in Denver, announced the President's condition as it had been told to him by Dr. Snyder.

Meanwhile Dr. Snyder calmly informed Mrs. Eisenhower of her husband's condition and telephoned Colonel Byron E. Pollock, chief of cardiology service at Fitzsimons General Hospital on the outskirts of Denver and told him to bring an electrocardiograph to the Doud house. The President began stirring about 11:45 A.M. When he was fully awake but still very weak, Dr. Snyder told him that he had summoned Dr. Pollock to take an electrocardiogram. Pollock arrived with Major General Martin E. Griffin, commanding general of the hospital, and they and Snyder made a tracing of the President's heart impulses.

The doctors took the tracing downstairs and laid it out on the dining-room table. It confirmed Snyder's diagnosis. A blood clot had blocked an artery in the front wall of the President's heart, cutting off the supply of blood from that part of the heart muscle. Snyder and Pollock returned to the President's bedroom. Snyder told Eisenhower that his heart had suffered an injury.

"We would like to take you to Fitzsimons," Snyder said.

The news did not seem to shock the President in the least, but, of course, he was still somewhat numbed from morphine.

"We're not going to get an ambulance," Snyder said.

"All right, Howard," the President replied, "call Jim"—James J. Rowley, chief of the White House Secret Service detail—"and get my car and let's go out."

Sergeant Moaney, his valet, helped the President into a bathrobe, and the three doctors supported him walking down the stairs, taking as much of his weight on their shoulders as they could manage. They had decided that it would be less of a strain on the President to walk down in this fashion than to be strapped to a stretcher and tipped in the air at the sharp angle that would have been required to carry him down the steep and narrow stairs, rounding the small halfway landing.

A limousine had been backed into the driveway, and on the porch two sturdy Secret Service men, Rowley and Deeter B. Flohr, Eisenhower's chauffeur, took over from the doctors and supported the President down the steps and into the rear of the car. Snyder sat on one side of the President and Pollock on the other. General Griffin slipped into a jump seat. With Flohr at the wheel and Rowley beside him they pulled away from the Doud house and made the nine-mile drive to the hospital at moderate speed. At Fitzsimons the car rolled up under a rear portico where a wheel chair was waiting to carry the President to the elevator. He smiled at the attendants in the corridor and had a friendly word for Charles Adams, the elevator operator who brought him up the eighth floor to a special suite with cream-colored walls, light-green furniture and green drapes. As soon as he slipped into bed, an oxygen tent was placed over the upper half of his body.

Then the news was broken to the world. Shortly after 2:30 P.M. Murray Snyder turned the press room at Lowry into bedlam with the announcement: "The President has just a mild anterior—let's cut out the word 'anterior'—the President has just had a mild coronary thrombosis. He has just been taken to Fitzsimons General Hospital. He was taken to the hospital in his own car and walked from the house to the car."

Dr. Snyder had notified him about 2 P.M. that the President was suffering from a mild anterior coronary thrombosis—after examination in the hospital "mild" was changed to "moderate"—but the assistant press secretary, who is an experienced newspaperman, felt that the word "anterior" in the initial announcement might cause confusion.

Before the announcement Snyder had called Hagerty, who was back in Washington on vacation, and told him what had happened.

"Jim, I intend to play this straight," he said, "and give the fellows everything as fast as we can get it."

"Right," Hagerty replied. "Give it to them absolutely straight. I'll catch a plane out as soon as I can."

Twelve hours had elapsed between the heart attack and the disclosure of his true condition, but from that moment on Murray Snyder, Hagerty and the doctors kept the people informed of the President's condition with thoroughness and candor.

When Hagerty learned of the attack shortly after 5 o'clock in the afternoon in Washington, he telephoned the Vice-President at the latter's white brick house in the fashionable Spring Valley section of Washington. Nixon had read in the *Evening Star* that the President was suffering from a digestive upset, and accepted at face value the report that his condition was not serious.

"Dick, I've got some bad news for you," Hagerty told him. "I've had a call from Murray Snyder in Denver. The President has had a coronary."

"Oh, my God!" Nixon gasped.

When the Vice-President could catch his breath, he told Hagerty that often heart attacks were not severe and that many patients enjoyed a complete recovery. Hagerty informed him that he was flying to Denver. He urged Nixon always to let him know where he could be reached.

Earlier Dr. Snyder had sent to Washington for Colonel Thomas M. Mattingly, the leading heart specialist at Walter Reed Hospital, who had the records on Eisenhower's heart dating back to 1946. Hagerty got in touch with Dr. Mattingly, a man on whose judgment the President came to place great reliance, and together they flew to Denver in an Air Force Constellation, arriving at 11:46 P.M. At the hospital Dr. Snyder told Hagerty that the President was glad he had returned to Denver. Snyder also quoted Eisenhower as having said, "Tell Jim to take over and make the decisions—and handle the story." Hagerty does not agree with an interpretation that has been placed upon these words that the

President was delegating to him the authority to run the executive branch of the government even temporarily. What Eisenhower meant, in his opinion, was that he should carry on his normal duties as press secretary. The fact remains, however, that as the senior White House official on the scene for several days and as the President's only authorized spokesman, he was in a position of authority far greater than is customarily exercised by the press secretary. Indeed it is difficult to think of anyone whose authority in those first couple of days exceeded that of Hagerty, a very surefooted official with a large capacity and a readiness to make decisions.

II

Nixon went dead inside after receiving Hagerty's call, he said afterward. For several minutes the Vice-President sat alone in his living room numbed by the possible implications of the President's attack. Presently he returned to the telephone and called his intimate friend Deputy Attorney General William P. Rogers, who had already heard the news, and asked him to come over. Rogers joined the Nixons for dinner, but with the telephone ringing constantly and newspapermen massing outside clamoring for a word with the Vice-President, it was next to impossible to carry on a conversation. Nixon suggested that they go to Rogers's house in nearby Bethesda, Maryland. Mrs. Rogers drove over to pick them up. To give the slip to reporters the Vice-President and Rogers ducked out a side door and scampered along an alley to another street where, by prearrangment, Mrs. Rogers was waiting.

After reaching his house Rogers telephoned General Persons, who, since Adams was in Europe winding up a vacation, was the senior officer on the White House staff. Persons had been notified of the heart attack by Hagerty before the press secretary took off for Denver. Rogers suggested that Persons join him and Nixon, and when the three of them got together later in the evening they had a long discussion. Nixon took the lead in urging, for example, that the Administration should show the world that the business of government was being carried on in the usual manner, with the members of the Cabinet and the White House staff going ahead with their normal duties within the framework of policies that had been laid out in the Cabinet and the N.S.C. After checking their opinion with Hagerty and other officials by telephone, the three agreed upon this course.

In a rather general way they speculated on the effect of Eisenhower's heart attack on national politics, particularly on the 1956 Presidential election. They agreed again after sounding out others, that it would be best for Administration officials not to make any public comments on this subject whatever until it was known how well the President would recover.

Reflecting the judgment that had been reached, Nixon made a statement to reporters after church the next morning, a Sunday, saying, "The business of government will go on without delay. . . . Under the President's administration a team has been set up in Washington which will carry out his well-defined plans."

In line with this display of "business as usual," four Administration officials, including Dulles and Humphrey, went to Ottawa, as planned, that Sunday to attend the United States–Canadian Joint Economic Conference. By prearrangement with Nixon the two Secretaries issued statements that the Administration would keep its stride in spite of the President's illness.

Late Sunday, Nixon, Persons and Rogers again met at Rogers' house, and during their discussion Nixon leaned to the opinion that he ought to call a meeting of the Cabinet for the following Friday. (Although a meeting of the N.S.C. had previously been set for Thursday, no Cabinet meeting was scheduled for the week.) He made the point that the gathering of the Cabinet might have the effect of demonstrating the orderly functioning of the government. He felt, however, that other members of the Cabinet should be consulted for their opinion, and no final decision was made that night.

Meanwhile that same day in Denver Hagerty had indicated that the Attorney General's office would be asked for a legal opinion as to whether during his illness certain of the President's powers might be delegated to others. His remark was in answer to a question about the signing of papers that are ordinarily brought to the President. Speculation was rife at the time on the possibility of having an "acting President" who would exercise temporarily some of the Constitutional powers of the President. Actually, Hagerty never asked the Attorney General for an opinion, and none was ever given on this point of delegation of Constitutional powers.

On Monday, however, Rogers, as acting Attorney General while Brownell vacationed in Spain, ordered a study on a related but fundamentally different question. This was whether the President while laid up could delegate his ministerial or non-Constitutional powers to one or more of his subordinates by executive order. Under such an arrangement there would be no question of an "acting President" or of the President's transferring authority specifically reserved to him by law.

That Monday—a day the stock market took its worst plunge since the Great Depression—Sherman Adams arrived from Europe aboard General Gruenther's plane. At noon he had luncheon at the White House with the Vice-President, Persons, and Rogers. While they were together, word arrived from Denver on the result of the first examination of Eisenhower by the Boston heart specialist Dr. Paul Dudley White, who in ensuing weeks was to become almost as famous as his patient. His verdict was that the President's condition was satisfactory and his morale high, that "conceivably" he could resume conferences within two weeks and should be ready to take up his normal activity after a couple of months. He even made the point under questioning that if Eisenhower enjoyed a good recovery, he would be physically able to run for President again if he wished. This news made it less likely that the question of delegation of non-Constitutional powers would have to be put up to the President.

The next day the idea of the executive order was dropped during a luncheon in the Secretary of the Treasury's office, attended by Humphrey, Nixon, Adams, Persons, Rogers, and Brownell, who had cut short his vacation. It was unnecessary, Brownell explained later, because the news from Denver "is encouraging."

There was a further reason. This was that no papers of any great consequence awaited the President's signature. A key to the whole problem was the fact that his illness struck at the lowest period of government activity. Congress had adjourned. The President had acted on all bills requiring his attention. The Big Four Foreign Ministers' meeting was still nearly a month away. Many high officials had just got off on vacation. Preparation of the major messages to be submitted by the President to Congress in January was in the earliest stages. Even if he had been in the best of health, it was a time when the President's participation in the routine business of government would have been at a minimum.

While consideration of delegation of powers was dropped, the idea of a Cabinet session on September 30 was approved.

III

The meeting was historic. The President lay in the hospital in Denver 1,551 miles away, improving but still not out of danger. Nixon, wearing a dark double-breasted suit, walked slowly into the Cabinet room with a serious air and took his place in the Vice-

President's chair between Humphrey on his right and Brownell on his left. Opposite Nixon was the empty chair of the President. As there was no agenda, the polished table was largely uncluttered with papers. The room, however, was cluttered with officials—thirty-four of them in addition to the Cabinet had crowded in and were banked around the white walls and the windows facing the rose garden.

At 9:30 A.M. the Vice-President called the meeting to order and asked for silent prayer. After a minute or so he broke the hush to read the morning medical bulletin from Denver. It said that the President had had an "excellent" night, sleeping almost uninterruptedly for nine and a half hours. It had been his first night out of the oxygen tent.

Nixon then looked to the Secretary of State for a review of the problems which faced the United States in foreign relations while the President was ill.

Dulles said that the most critical situation at the moment was the Middle East. In Cyprus, he said, the situation was inflamed. The Cypriots were demonstrating against British rule in their movement for union with Greece, and the disorder carried a threat to the Mediterranean flank of NATO. Dulles explained the United States had decided to support the British in voting to keep the Cyprus question off the agenda of the U.N. General Assembly mainly to give tensions a chance to ease in hopes that a gradual settlement could be reached.

The Soviet Union's decision to furnish arms to Egypt was also causing a critical problem, Dulles continued. He warned that the Soviet move threatened the peace between Egypt and Israel. The flow of arms, he said, might carry into other areas of Africa. Without giving any details, he assured the Cabinet that the United States was not without plans for dealing with the situation.

Dulles said that the talks between the United States and Red Chinese ambassadors in Geneva were not going well at the moment because, for possibly ulterior motives, the Chinese seemed to be reneging on the release of American civilians.

On the bright side he reported that talks among Americans, British and French in New York in preparation for the Foreign Ministers' conference in Geneva had gone splendidly.

Nixon then directed the attention of the members to the heart of the matter before the Cabinet—the plans for running the government in the President's absence.

Government affairs, he said at the outset, should be carried on with dispatch. Routine matters must not get piled up in a logjam awaiting the President's return. Nixon said that actions taken by the government should be within the framework of policies established by the President. One important way of doing this, he pointed out, was to channel important measures through the Cabinet or the N.S.C.

The Vice-President reserved for future decision by the President the establishment of important new policies.

He made certain suggestions for the carrying out of existing policies. Departments and agencies should proceed as usual in conduct of business which was strictly in their jurisdiction. In the case of other actions which ordinarily are submitted in advance to the Cabinet as a matter of courtesy, this practice should continue. On the preceding day, he said, the N.S.C. had decided that those actions in the Council's field which customarily are taken only after discussion with the President should now, during his illness, be reviewed in the N.S.C. in lieu of or as preliminary to discussions with the President. The Cabinet, Nixon said, might wish to decide upon a procedure to be followed with respect to its actions.

No immediate problem of conducting the government presented itself, he continued, because it now appeared that the President would soon be allowed by his doctors to sign routine papers. He said it was fortunate that the President had established an effective team that could—he quoted Dulles's statement of the preceding Sunday—carry on "the policies and principles" of the Administration without harm to "the steady prosecution of our national and international policies." Nixon said that it was very important to keep the public aware that this was the Eisenhower Administration and not the Administration of any other person or group.

Brownell said that he saw no legal barrier to prevent the Cabinet from following the procedure agreed upon by the N.S.C. He went on to say that he was sure that all members would wish to lean over backward to make sure that no actions by their respective agencies affecting other agencies or the general policy of the Administration would be taken without prior discussion in the Cabinet or the N.S.C.

The Attorney General had been asked, he said, to determine how the burden of purely routine actions might be lightened for the President. (Evidently this was a reference to the study ordered by Rogers on Monday.) Brownell suggested that each Cabinet officer prepare a list of actions in his particular department requiring Presidential approval and of suggestions as to which types of action might be handled by someone other than the President. Brownell said that certain duties had often been delegated by Presidents in the past. More could be in the future, Rowland Hughes observed.

The Attorney General read the draft of a statement he had been asked by the N.S.C. to prepare on the conduct of the government in the weeks ahead. The Cabinet suggested several changes in wording and agreed that it should be issued after the meeting by Murray Snyder, who had returned from Denver. The statement, in part, read:

> After full discussion of pending matters, it was concluded that there are no obstacles to the orderly and uninterrupted conduct of the foreign and domestic affairs of the nation during the period of rest ordered by the President's physicians.
>
> Governor Sherman Adams, the Assistant to the President, will leave for Denver today and will be available there, in consultation with the President's physicians, whenever it may later become appropriate to present any matters to the President.
>
> The policies and programs of the Administration as determined and approved by the President are well established along definite lines and are well known. Co-ordination of the activities of the several departments of the government within the framework of these policies will be continued by full co-operation among the responsible officers of these departments so that the functions of the government will be carried forward in an effective manner during the absence of the President.

Brownell and Humphrey both said it would be a good idea for members to refrain from public comment on this statement. The Secretary of the Treasury appealed for co-operation among departments and for frank thrashing out of complicated problems in the Cabinet and the N.S.C. so that in the coming weeks there would be no appearance of controversy within the Administration.

Adams said that he had talked to Dr. White the evening before and that it was agreed that the doctors should determine at any given time whether routine documents might be submitted to the President for his approval. In this early stage of convalescence, Adams added, it also was agreed that the President should not be handed controversial issues or papers requiring such close attention as to tax his strength.

Stassen told the Cabinet he thought that effective teamwork in the days ahead would offer the highest tribute the members could pay to the President's ability in organizing the government and selecting capable subordinates. Summerfield asked about keeping speaking engagements during the President's illness. Humphrey said that this did pose a problem, but he felt that members should live up to their speaking commitments. He considered it important that such speeches should be confined to the Administration's record and not calculated to arouse partisan controversy. The Cabinet agreed with Humphrey's suggestions.

Nixon reminded the Cabinet that questions were bound to arise about the outlook for the Republican Party. He suggested that they should be brushed right off as unworthy of discussion when the national concern was for the President's recovery. He also suggested that speakers might comment upon Eisenhower's skill in having formed an effective administrative machine.

Adams said that Dr. White had heard someone suggest that the President issue a public statement and that the doctor offered no objection. Benson and Lodge remarked that if and when such a statement was issued, it should express thanks for the many prayers being offered throughout the world for the President's recovery.

Howard Pyle, one of the President's administrative assistants, interposed to urge again that speeches during this period avoid controversy and emphasize that business was going on as usual. The President's illness, he said, did not make it necessary for members of the Administration to reject speaking engagements.

Dulles reminded the Cabinet that in Denver, Adams would be the channel for presentations to the President. The Secretary observed that some individuals outside government (he mentioned no names) might presume authoritatively to reflect the President's opinions. This was all the more reason, he continued, to strengthen the position of Adams, who was already a highly respected national figure. Nixon seconded this and noted that in Adams's absence Persons would be senior at the White House. Government business should be channeled through the White House staff in the usual manner, he added.

Persons urged Cabinet members to assume responsibility for holding in their departments papers not requiring early action rather than allowing them to pile up in the White House, making it appear that the President's absence was impeding routine business. Nixon agreed with this and said it did not conflict with the plans already discussed for routing policy matters through the Cabinet and the N.S.C. He said that the Attorney General would have to take on the additional task of keeping an eye on any special legal problems that might arise under current conditions.

The discussion on operations of the government in Eisenhower's absence ended with a word from Kevin McCann on the desirability of co-ordinating speeches.

A few items of minor business were discussed.

Approval was given to Adams's suggestion for forming a Cabinet committee on the highway program.

Mitchell reported on plans for the National Conference on Equal Economic Opportunity. He digressed to say that an expert on racial relations under the Truman Administration had offered high praise privately for the manner in which the Eisenhower Administration was dealing with this problem.

There was talk on implementing Hoover Commission recommendations and on the state of the economy. Humphrey observed that even if the highway program was approved at the 1956 session of Congress, the economy would not feel the effect for another year or two. Hughes said that a "fine spirit" of co-operation had been evident since the last session when the President had set a goal of reducing expenditures by 3 per cent. Even without any economies in the Defense Department, Hughes said, he was hopeful that spending would drop by $700,000,000.

Departments were preparing to submit material for inclusion in the State of the Union message. Adams recalled that the President had once voiced his hope that some day he could deliver a "twenty-minute message." Adams hoped that departments would be very concise in their submissions this year.

At noon the meeting ended. Noting that Nixon had been under immense strain during the last week, Dulles closed the discussion by expressing on behalf of the Cabinet appreciation for the manner in which the Vice-President had conducted himself.

IV

In Denver the President's recovery continued without complications. Letters and telegrams poured into the hospital by the tens of thousands. Bags of mail piled up in an auditorium, and on her visits to the President, Mrs. Eisenhower, who was living in the hospital, would drop by and scoop up an armful and take them into his room and read samples to him. The note that predominated was that people were praying for him. This seemed to have a deeply heartening effect on Eisenhower. Over and over again he kept telling his visitors how much he was moved by the prayers and sympathy of the people for a stricken President.

"It really does something for you to know that people all over the world are praying for you," he said to Mrs. Eisenhower one day after she had finished reading some messages.

A little thing that did a great deal for the President's morale was the uncharacteristically gaudy costume the newspapermen sent him on his sixty-fifth birthday on October 14. It consisted of bright-red pajamas with a general of the Army's five stars embroidered in gold on each collar tab and MUCH BETTER, THANKS embroidered over the breast pocket. Setting off the pajamas was a glossy black Western tie with silver sequins, which Merriman Smith and Laurence H. Burd, of the Chicago *Tribune*, bought for thirty-nine cents. Day in and day out, the President wore this getup around the hospital in a mood approaching hilarity, and the doctors encouraged him to wear it.

Mrs. Eisenhower and her son ordered records of the President's favorite music for reading and relaxation.*

On September 30 the President resumed his official duties by initialing two lists of recess appointments of foreign-service officers. Two days later it was announced that the President was "a little tired," and the news shook the stock market, sending leading shares down by from one to five points and reducing the total value of stocks on the New York Stock Exchange by four billion dollars. But the President bounced back and so did the market, and little by little as the days passed Eisenhower devoted more attention to government business. One after another, Cabinet officers and other leading officials came to Denver.

Partly these visits were intended as demonstrations of the President's continuing authority and of his gradual resumption of active direction of the government. Also, it has been pointed out, the press conferences at which these official visitors reported on their talks with Eisenhower constituted a form of communication between the stricken President and the people. But there was also

* They included *"Clair de lune,"* Drigo's "Serenade," "Greensleeves," "Festival," "Dream of Olwen," "Song of Love," "Flirtation Waltz," *"Matinata," "Amoureuse,"* "To a Wild Rose," "Serenade in the Night," "Barcarole," "In the Still of the Night," "Stardust," "Moonlight and Roses," "Sleepy Lagoon," "Indian Summer," "Drink to Me Only With Thine Eyes." Also a melody from *Die Fledermaus,* "Caucasian Love Song," a melody from *Countess Maritza, "Toujours l'amour,"* "Songs My Mother Taught Me," a melody from *The Gypsy Baron,* "The Old Refrain" and a medley from *The Student Prince.* There were also these songs played by Al Goodman and his orchestra: "One Alone," "Time on My Hands," the entr'acte and intermezzo from *The Chocolate Soldier,* "Deep in My Heart," Beethoven's Minuet Number 2 in G, "The Funeral March of a Marionette," Schumann's "Nocturne," "Will You Remember?" and a medley from *The Merry Widow.*

another important side to these calls, and that was their therapeutic purpose. A sense of participation, of being able to discharge his responsibilities, was increasingly important to the President's morale and health, as it would have been in the case of any coronary patient.

Dr. Snyder and Dr. White soon became aware that Eisenhower was lying in bed thinking about government problems. These thoughts often escaped in his talks with them. White told Adams and Hagerty that it would be beneficial for the President to receive Cabinet officers. In the early stages their talks dealt with less exacting problems, but as time went on the doctors would buttonhole visiting officials before they went into the President's room and tell them to speak to him straight from the shoulder and not act as if they were addressing someone on his deathbed.

"Look," White told Hagerty, "he's not so much of an invalid as he is the President of the United States lying in there. He wants to do his job."

Indeed, Eisenhower himself began to cut down on his callers' glowing words of greeting and urge that they get down to business.

Toward the end of October the President was able to take hold of a problem for an hour without ill effect. Adams, as usual, was the channel through which work flowed to and from Eisenhower, and in this period the influence of the Assistant to the President upon the operations of the government was very considerable. Working in a plain office on the second floor of the administration building at Lowry overlooking a parking lot, Adams was on the phone to Washington from morning until night, giving instructions, arranging conferences, summoning officials to see the President and making innumerable administrative decisions. He would lay out areas of policy in which the President alone must make decisions and then see to it that decisions were reached on matters beyond these boundaries. In Denver, as in Washington, his authority was enhanced by his unique prerogative in speaking for the President—"It is the President's wish that . . ." or "The President hopes you will . . ." and so forth.

Each week Adams would fly to Washington to attend meetings of the Cabinet and N.S.C. These sessions reflected many of the problems and activities of the government during the President's convalescence.

CABINET, OCTOBER 7, 1955

Adams brought word that the President was making excellent progress and with each day was more eager to get back on the job. The medical experts believed, Adams continued, that Eisenhower could soon take part in government affairs. After Nixon had noted that the President's birthday was only a week off, it was agreed that Adams should arrange for a birthday present from the Cabinet.

Benson brought up the farm problem and remarked that it would be an issue in the 1956 campaign. The agricultural surplus which the Administration had inherited, he said, was a "time bomb," and he urged all high officials to close ranks to support the farm policy in 1956, as they had done in the 1954 campaign.

The Secretary presented a paper on the problem, which said that the farm situation was not likely to improve in the next twelve months. Farm income had declined some 20 per cent from its peak in 1951, second year of the Korean war, although the per capita income of all farmers from all sources had dropped but 6 per cent. The billions of dollars' worth of government-held surpluses took the buoyancy out of the market. The surplus couldn't be dumped in the ocean or sold quickly at any price or given away soon, the report went on. The commodities must be disposed of gradually. In spite of hardships, the report said, the status of the farmer was fundamentally sound as measured by working capital, reserves, land values, and the ratio of debts to assets.

The report discussed the political aspects of the problem. The fortunes of the farmer had waned during the years the Administration had been in office. The report put the blame on the difficulty of readjusting from a wartime to a peacetime economy, on what it called the bad farm law which the Eisenhower Administration had inherited and the "irresponsible" decisions of the Truman Administration. The problem, it said, was to make the people see through the "demagoguery" being practiced by the Democrats over the farm situation. Republican leaders, recalling the disaster of the 1948 campaign, were uneasy, and Democrats were trying to arouse dissatisfaction in the Midwest, capitalizing on the decline in the price of hogs.

Finally, the report suggested these measures: appropriation of perhaps $200,000,000 to help farmers turn land unsuited to crops into grass or forest; approval for farmers to grow wheat for their own use without any restrictions; assistance to the cotton market; readiness to help the market for hogs, potatoes, and perishable foods through a limited program of government purchases; support of farm prices at the highest level that would be possible without causing undue acquisition by the government of further surpluses.

The paper urged strong support of the White House and the Republican National Committee for Benson's farm policy.

Summerfield asked if it would not be a good idea to begin purchasing hogs immediately because of current low prices. Benson replied that it was a matter of timing. (On October 24 he launched an $85,000,000 program for purchase of pork and lard.) The Postmaster General said that on travels across the country he had found respect for Benson and the farm program, but a feeling notwithstanding that the Department of Agriculture was not sympathetic to the farmer in times of crisis.

Stassen recalled things the Administration had done to restore the economy in the recession of 1953-54 and argued that the farm problem should be tackled now with the same determination. While approving the economic soundness of the steps outlined in Benson's report, he suggested that, in addition, more dramatic strokes were necessary to give the program political appeal. He also emphasized that the price of hogs must be turned upward before it hit rock bottom. For the problem as a whole, he urged measures to reduce the number of farms and for selling commodities abroad. In short, he favored a long-range program plus immediate "crisis" measures.

As the meeting progressed, the farm program came under increasing questioning. Stassen suggested that the heavy sums used to store surpluses might be put to better use retiring land from cultivation. Wilson noted that irrigation and fertilizer programs were creating more surpluses. Brownell observed that Benson's report led to the conclusion that the farm situation would not have bettered by the fall of 1956 (when the Presidential campaign would be on), and he also contrasted this with the improvement that had been achieved in the industrial situation in the preceding year. Benson said that at least the farm situation would remain steady, but he warned that no quick solution was in sight. Brownell reminded the Cabinet that troubles on the farm were standing out in contrast to good times in the city.

Humphrey questioned whether a great deal could be done about the farm problem except to let natural processes do their work. As for the recession, he said that the things the Administration did were without great effect. The important fact, he argued, was that the administration had established confidence in the minds of the people that it would not try all sorts of manipulations with the economy. There was no panacea for the farm problem and the

Administration should not panic in the face of the situation, Humphrey said. The Secretary was not sure that business would continue to be as good in 1956 as it was in 1955.

Dulles cautioned against any thought of dumping surpluses abroad because of the resentment this would cause among our allies.

Secretary McKay was convinced that planned economy does not work. The country, he said, would be in the best possible shape when it could return to private enterprise unfettered by bureaucratic interference. He cited, for example, the natural shift in usages of land to meet changes in the price of commodities. He advocated a return to the fundamentals of the Constitution.

As the presiding officer, Nixon summarized the discussion. It showed, he said, no disagreement on the soundness of the long-range program outlined in Benson's report and agreement on the necessity for seeking additional measures. The Vice-President said he was sure the Cabinet recognized the political implications of the problem and the significance of Brownell's points. It was important, Nixon concluded, that the Administration should arouse hope for improvement among the farmers and publicize the actions it was taking to better conditions.

Adams said that before his illness Eisenhower had shown a deep interest in this problem.

CABINET, OCTOBER 14, 1955

At Nixon's suggestion the Cabinet tape-recorded a birthday greeting to the President.

Adams reported that the preceding day the President had told the doctors it was his best since becoming ill. The President was anxious to get back into the swing of things, and numerous matters were now being discussed with him. During one of these conferences the President said he believed that the number of Federal employees was still too high. He felt that the number of new employees being hired by the government could be cut by perhaps a hundred thousand, and he asked Adams to relay his views to the Cabinet.

Reporting on his twenty-five-minute call at the hospital, Dulles had found the President's mind fresh and vigorous and had come away feeling that Eisenhower was ready to apply himself to any problem that might become acute.

Arthur Burns presented a program for assistance to depressed areas. An Agency for Area Development would be established in the Department of Commerce to provide technical assistance and make loans to assist local rehabilitation plans. Federal participation would be modest and the states would co-operate as partners.

Weeks questioned the creation of a new lending agency, and Humphrey cautioned against loans to perpetuate or bring into existence industries that were uneconomic and could not withstand certain inevitable changes. This would amount to taxing thriving concerns to subsidize potential rivals at considerable risk to the government, he said. Wilson, recalling his "bird dog" remark, asked whether it was sound to attempt artificially to stimulate activity in a particular area when it served no natural purpose. Stassen said that something should be done, perhaps with experimentation first through a "pilot plant." Humphrey agreed, as did Nixon. The Vice-President summarized the discussion as producing agreement that some program was necessary but that further study was required. (In Denver on October 24 the President gave "strong approval" to plans for introducing the Burns program in the next Congress.)

Nixon said that on his recent visit to Denver the President had asked him to carry back word that he was proud of the manner in which the Cabinet was carrying on in his absence. Eisenhower told the Vice-President he was sure that in the whole of American history there had never been another Cabinet like this one.

(During the President's convalescence Rabb sent Eisenhower summaries of Cabinet proceedings.)

CABINET, OCTOBER 21, 1955

Adams said that the President's interest in government affairs and his activity continued to increase. Particularly, Adams recounted the President's air of confidence and his optimism about the future. Eisenhower wished to get started with his work on the State of the Union message, Adams reported.

Dulles discussed the agenda of the forthcoming Geneva meeting of the Big Four Foreign Ministers. He said the conference might be successful if it could undertake a discussion of the German question, which the Soviets were anxious to avoid. He reported that he had discussed the conference with the President and with Congressional leaders. The leaders, he said, had given him their support.

The Vice-President then read the following letter:

Denver, Colorado
October 19, 1955

Dear Dick:

I want to say a word to you, and through you to my Cabinet associates, about the task which Foster Dulles will be assuming at Geneva. As head of the American Delegation he will be carrying a heavy load of responsibility, not only as Secretary of State, but as my personal representative having my complete confidence and with whom I have continuous close understanding.

This second meeting at Geneva was one of the steps toward solving the world problems which Foster and I planned together and which we have talked over fully not only before my illness, but twice since.

I hope that each one in Government will do whatever he can to make Foster's task easier. The Secretary of State must have the discretionary authority which is needed if there is to be effective negotiation and the spirit of conciliation which I have called for at that meeting. He must be the one who both at the conference table and before the world speaks for me with authority for our country.

With warm regard,

As ever,
DWIGHT D. EISENHOWER

The Vice-President
Washington, D. C.

CABINET, OCTOBER 28, 1955

Reporting on the President's progress, Adams said that Eisenhower should be able to participate in Cabinet and N.S.C. meetings by the end of the year.

Mitchell outlined the proposed legislation the Department of Labor expected to submit to Congress and said, in answer to a question by Brownell, that it would not include any recommendation for making unions subject to the antitrust laws. It would include the amendments to the Taft-Hartley Act unsuccessfully proposed in 1954 and 1955. Mitchell talked of the possibility of extending greater recognition to unions of government employees. Summerfield did not think this was a good idea.

Nixon said that public opinion polls showed that increasingly workers felt that the Republican Party served their interest best in economic affairs. The Democrats had slipped slightly in these samplings, he told the Cabinet.

Weeks reviewed studies of the recently established Cabinet committee on the highway program. The Administration's plan for financing new highways by bonds outside the debt limit had been dropped, he said, in favor of raising money by new or increased taxes on gasoline and tires and higher excises on trucks and buses. Weeks desired to present this program at the meeting of the highway committee of the governors' conference, scheduled for November 3.

Humphrey agreed with these recommendations. He felt very strongly, he said, that he had erred the previous spring in testifying in favor of the bond issue. He realized now, he went on, that Congress could not enter into an agreement to commit revenues from certain taxes to particular purposes over a future period and thus the proposed bonds would have been backed only by the good faith of the government and general revenues. Adams asked for assurances—and received them—that under the new plan revenues from the increased taxes would be devoted in entirety to the highway program to ward off opposition from the states. The Cabinet approved submission of the committee's recommendations to the governors' committee.

The Postmaster General presented the case for increased postal rates. Nixon was doubtful whether the Administration should blow up a storm over this issue in the election-year session. As a possible course he suggested that Summerfield seek a way of getting action on this issue without incurring the sharp opposition of the Democratic leaders. Stassen said that perhaps Summerfield could obtain Democratic support for establishment of a bipartisan commission to fix rates and thus remove this business from the field of politics. Summerfield felt sure that Speaker Rayburn would not go along with this idea. The Cabinet agreed that further study should be given to the final position the Administration would take on postal rates. (On February 1, 1956, the President asked Congress to increase rates so as to bring in an additional $406,000,000. Three-cent stamps would go to four cents and airmail stamps from six to seven cents.)

After nearly seven weeks in the hospital the President was discharged on November 11 and headed back to Washington immediately. At the airport in Denver he made a brief speech thanking those who had sent him messages and prayed for him. "Misfortune, and particularly the misfortune of illness," he said, "brings to all of us an understanding of how good people are." That same afternoon thousands turned out in Washington to welcome him home.

As he stepped off the plane in his familiar tan polo coat and brown snap-brim hat he was greeted by Nixon and former President Hoover. "I am happy the doctors have given me at least a parole, if not a pardon," Eisenhower said, "and I expect to be back at my accustomed duties, although they say I must ease my way into 'em and not bulldoze my way into them."

After a long weekend in the White House during which he began taking practice swings again with his golf clubs on the south lawn, he drove to Gettysburg with Mrs. Eisenhower on November 14 to resume convalescence at his farm on the edge of the battlefield. Lincoln Square was jammed with seven thousand people who sang and cheered the Eisenhowers when they arrived. The square was hung with banners and placards reading GLAD YOU'RE HOME, IKE and WELCOME HOME, IKE AND MAMIE.

The President attended his first Cabinet meeting since his illness on November 22. It was held in trim, rustic Laurel Cottage on the mountainside at Camp David. As the meeting was breaking up, the President asked all members to wait so that he could take this chance to thank them and his staff for the way they had conducted themselves in his absence. For five weeks after his attack, he recalled, he had not seen a newspaper. However, he was shown an editorial expressing surprise that the Cabinet and staff had worked so well together under the circumstances. Perhaps, the President laughed, there might even have been a few hints that the Cabinet did better without him.

The only thing that surprised him, he went on, was that the editorial writer should have expressed surprise that the Cabinet worked harmoniously and successfully in following the Administration's familiar and practicable middle course between the extremes of too little and too much. He knew, he said, that the Cabinet could carry on because of the dedication of the members to this policy at home and abroad.

The events of recent weeks, Eisenhower said, gave him pride in the choices he had made for members of his Cabinet and staff. He expressed his gratitude for their conduct. This Cabinet, he thought, was unique. He recalled that as long ago as George Washington's Administration strife had rent the Cabinet while Hamilton and Jefferson were both members of it. No other Cabinet, in his opinion, had ever been so completely dedicated to a set of broad principles upon which all could work together. He was glad of the chance for putting this to the test. He added, however, that he had not relished the particular circumstances that brought it about.

JAMES TOBIN

The Eisenhower Economy and National Security: Defense, Dollars, and Doctrines

THE FORCE of ideas in history has never been better described than in the famous concluding passage of John Maynard Keynes's *General Theory of Employment, Interest, and Money*: ". . . the ideas of economists and political philosophers, both when they are right and when they are wrong, are more powerful than is commonly understood. Indeed the world is ruled by little else. Practical men, who believe themselves to be quite exempt from any intellectual influences, are usually the slaves of some defunct economist. Madmen in authority, who hear voices in the air, are distilling their frenzy from some academic scribbler of a few years back. I am sure that the power of vested interests is vastly exaggerated compared with the gradual encroachment of ideas. Not, indeed, immediately, but after a certain interval; for in the field of economic and political philosophy there are not many who are influenced by new theories after they are twenty-five or thirty years of age, so that the ideas which civil servants and politicians and even agitators apply to current events are not likely to be the newest. But, soon or late, it is ideas, not vested interests, which are dangerous for good or evil."

The recent economic policies of the United States government provide a dramatic confirmation of Keynes's high estimate of the power of economic ideology. In this instance the ideas have been dangerous for evil; the policies they have dictated have cost the United States its world leadership and gravely threatened its survival as a nation. The central doctrine of the economic philosophy that has produced this disaster is very simple: Government inter-

"The Eisenhower Economy and National Security: Defense, Dollars, and Doctrines" by James Tobin is from the March 1958 issue of *The Yale Review*.

vention in economic life—spending, taxing, borrowing, regulating —is an evil to be minimized; man's needs are best accommodated, and progress is most rapid, when private enterprise flourishes unfettered by government regulations and unburdened by the dead weight of government activity. This economic philosophy has a long and honorable tradition, going back to Adam Smith (*Wealth of Nations,* 1776) and the classical economists of the nineteenth century. Throughout much of their history, classical economic ideas have been a power for good. As the intellectual basis for the liberation of economic life from feudal restrictions and from provincial and national barriers to trade, they assisted in the industrial transformation of the Western World in the past century and a half. At other times, however, the doctrine of minimal government has been singularly inappropriate. Twice in this century men of strong and sincere devotion to this orthodox economic position have been in power in Washington at times when the situation cried out for expansion rather than limitation of federal activity and initiative.

Once was the depression of 1929-32, when the stern principles and strong character of President Hoover shaped the economic policies of the federal government. Against common sense, against his own humanitarian instincts, against strong political pressures, Herbert Hoover refused to use the power and purse of the federal government to aid the victims of the Great Depression. His stubborn adherence to principle was in a way admirable; unhappily the doctrines that commanded his devotion were 100 per cent wrong for the situation he confronted. The nation slid to the brink of revolution, from which it was saved less by the fact that Roosevelt had in the beginning any different economic views than by the fact that Roosevelt was a flexible and pragmatic politician.

Orthodox fiscal doctrines have again dominated our policies during the last five years, and again they have brought the nation to the brink of catastrophe, a different and infinitely more serious catastrophe than the internal collapse of 1932. We have had once again a businessman's administration, and once more it has been demonstrated that there is no one more doctrinaire and impractical in public affairs than some successful practical men of private affairs. This time it is not the President who has a firm and well-defined ideological position but the men on whom he has relied. The economic doctrines loyally held by former Secretary of the Treasury Humphrey, former Secretary of Defense Wilson, and Chairman Martin of the Federal Reserve have been the powerful determinants of the Administration's budgetary and monetary policies. In Congress leadership in both parties has passed to men of similar beliefs, such as Senators Johnson and Knowland. The climate of opinion since 1953 has given new power and prestige to the extreme anti-government views of Senator Byrd.

No decision of our government is more important, in the 1950's, than the decision how much of the vast productive resources of the nation to devote to the defense of the United States and of the free world. Defense must be broadly interpreted. In the short run, our security depends on the armaments we already have and the personnel we have to man them. In a longer view, it depends on our production of more armaments, and on our program of research and development of new weapons. In a still longer view, tomorrow's defense depends on today's support of basic science, including the education and recruitment of the ablest talent of the maturing generation. And both today and tomorrow, our security is inextricably wound up with the economic, social, and military health of our allies and with the progress of the uncommitted and underdeveloped nations of the world.

To all of these programs the federal budget is the key. It is no exaggeration to say that our defense policy, our foreign aid policy, and inevitably our entire foreign policy have been shaped by the men who have made our fiscal policy. Humphrey and Byrd have had more effect on our defense program and foreign policy than Dulles, or than Khrushchev.

A *New Yorker* cartoon in early September showed a middle-aged middle-class wife commenting to her husband: "It's a great week for everybody. The Russians have the intercontinental ballistic missile, and we have the Edsel." The major economic and foreign policy of the Administration could not be more succinctly expressed. The response of the Administration to the news in August, 1957, of Russia's success with missiles, which coincided with Russian diplomatic gains in Syria and the Arab world and with Russian intransigeance in disarmament negotiations, was a continuation of the vigorous effort of Secretary Wilson to *reduce* the rate of spending of the Defense Department by about four billion dollars a year. At a time when the world situation cried out for accelerating and enlarging our defense effort, the Administration *released* money, labor, scientific talent, materials, and plant capacity. Since the ramifications of Pentagon decisions on contracts, subcontracts, orders, and jobs take time, the economic consequences of the Wilson cutbacks are still being felt. It will also take time to reverse them.

Leave aside the confusions and distractions created by the mysteries of public finance and focus on the simple and basic economic question: In what uses other than unemployment were these released resources to be absorbed? For what more pressing purposes were these resources released? For research and development of new consumer luxuries, for new plants in which to produce more consumers' goods, old and new, all to be marketed by the most advanced techniques of mass persuasion to a people who already enjoy the highest and most frivolous standard of living in history.

The policies of Secretaries Humphrey and Wilson in 1957 were not new. A reduction in the federal government's share of the national output has always been a prime goal of the Administration, and its ascendant position in Humphrey's scale of values showed in his ill-concealed frustration and anger that the 1958 budget was still so big. No sooner was Eisenhower installed in power than the Administration grasped with enthusiasm the proposition that nuclear weapons made it possible to have "more bang for a buck," more military power at less cost. The doctrine of "massive retaliation" was made as much in Treasury as in State. The United States turned its back on the concept of limited wars, and on the maintenance of the costly manpower and conventional armaments necessary to be prepared to fight them. Taken seriously, the policy greatly reduces our freedom of action in case of local Communist aggression as in Korea. Lacking conventional arms, we can either precipitate a nuclear war with the Soviet Union or do nothing at all to oppose the aggression. The success of the policy as a deterrent depended on our maintaining a lead in nuclear weapons and the ability to deliver them. Now that lead has evaporated, perhaps been reversed. The same solicitude for the budget that has weakened us in conventional arms has enabled the Soviet Union to catch us and surpass us in the realm of nuclear weapons and rockets.

In the course of his two radio-TV addresses to the nation in defense of his budget in May, 1957, the President said that the defense and foreign aid budgets could not be reduced without taking "reckless gambles" with the security of the free world. Thus he in effect admitted that these budgets were already too low. We are much too rich a country to keep our defenses at the margin of taking very serious risks to our very survival. A nation on the edge of starvation might of necessity be on the edge of insecurity. The United States has no private uses of resources so compelling that they justify keeping the Western World in such a precarious position that any reduction in the budget will gravely threaten security. We can afford more of a cushion than that, and we can't afford not to have it.

For the defense of North America against nuclear attack from the air, the government has done almost nothing. In May, 1956, General Partridge, in command of continental air defense, testified before a Congressional committee that an adequate program —radar warning, interceptors, ground-to-air missiles, etc.—would cost 65 billion dollars over the fifteen-year period 1951-65, and that scarcely any of this amount had yet been spent. Our civil defense program, as everyone knows, is a joke. The federal government has put no money into it, and it is not something that state, localities, and private individuals can do for themselves. Casualties could be greatly diminished by shelters, but we have not even made a beginning in building them. Similarly, industrial decentralization has been pursued only in a half-hearted way; we favor decentralization as long as it costs nothing. Meanwhile its greater geographical concentration makes American industry a more vulnerable target than its Soviet counterpart. Underground installation of certain vital industrial plants may be essential for the nation to survive an attack, but this is another area where we evidently have no program.

The catalogue of unfilled defense needs could be extended to requirements of a less immediate military nature but of equal or greater ultimate importance. Assistance in the economic development of Africa, Asia, and Latin America, and support of all levels of education in the United States itself would be high on an extended list. But enough examples have been given to make the essential point. The unfilled needs of defense are great and they are urgent. Whether we wish to try to meet them depends on how we weigh in the balance the urgency of these defense needs against the urgency of those private uses of resources that would have to be sacrificed. Anyone who appraises the luxury standard of living of the United States with the perspective of historical comparisons or comparisons with the rest of the contemporary world will strike the balance only one way. He will prefer to save our lives rather than our leisure; he will value freedom over fashion.

If reasonable men nevertheless oppose expansion of government defense programs, they must have loaded the other side of the scales with weighty considerations beyond the intrinsic importance of maintaining and increasing the consumption level of our population. What are the weighty considerations that tip the scales for men like Secretary Humphrey and Senator Byrd? They come from the classical economic philosophy of these men, and they may be summarized in three fears: (1) fear of the national debt, (2) fear of the long-run effects of large government budgets and high tax rates on the productivity of the economy, and (3) fear of inflation. Unfortunately for the suitability of the recent policies of the government but fortunately for the nation and the world, there is not enough substance to any of these fears, individually or in combination, to prevent us from doing what needs to be done to defend the free world.

(1) The most pressing motivation for Secretary Wilson's heroic efforts at economy last summer was the 275 billion-dollar limit on the national debt, Senator Byrd's contribution to sound public finance. The Treasury feared that undiminished spending would pierce the 275 billion-dollar limit, at least temporarily until tax receipts roll in this spring. The Administration preferred taking two or three 100,000-man whacks at the armed forces to facing the ire with which Senator Byrd and his orthodox friends of both parties in Congress would greet a request to raise the debt limit. Even in 1958 the Treasury asks only for a temporary five-billion-dollar increase in the limit, and apologizes for that. If the United States is destroyed, the history books, if any, can record their pride that the debt limit was never breached.

Imagine a rich country, with an annual national income over 400 billion dollars a year, in debt to foreign countries to the tune of 275 billion dollars, paying eight billion dollars a year interest to its external creditors. A debt of this size would be no calamity. The interest burden would be well within the nation's capacity to pay, and there would be no reason for the country to cripple itself in time of need by an arbitrary self-imposed debt limit. But at least there would be some real burden, and it would be prudent for those who manage the nation's economic affairs to give thought to its external debt. The United States has no such debt; indeed we are a net creditor of the rest of the world. Senator Byrd's ordinance of self-denial applies to an internal debt. The people of the United States are both debtor and creditor. The eight billion dollars a year in interest is not a diversion of our production to foreigners. It is paid by us as taxpayers to us as bondholders (either directly or to banks, insurance companies, pension funds, and other institutions that invest our savings in government bonds.) Since the debt is, so to speak, within the family, its size can and should be the servant of public policy, not the master. Congress can in any case control the size of the debt by budgeting for surpluses or deficits as the occasion demands; the debt limit is quite superfluous, except for inhibiting the Treasury's ability to deal with seasonal variation in its disbursements and revenues. The debt limit represents a misdirected collective resolution to be good; its unchallenged appeal can only be based on semantic confusion. Under the debt limit, Uncle Sam fights with one hand tied behind his back, a handicap imposed neither by any necessity of nature nor any wile of his enemy, but by himself.

(2) Americans take comfort in the enormous productive power of the country, still far in advance of the Soviet Union. One of the orthodox arguments for minimal government is that the military strength of America and of the free world depends ultimately on this productive power and its continued growth. Twice the mobilization of America's productive power has saved the world, and if it is permitted to flourish and grow, this power will be our security once more. Our productive strength can be "sapped" and its growth arrested, we are told, by high government budgets, foreign aid, debt, taxation, and inflation. Then all will be lost.

This argument is wrong and dangerous, on several counts.

First, the revolution in the technology of destruction means that the next world war, if ever it comes, will be decided by forces in being, not by potential strength. The weapons that our factories *could* produce, our engineers *could* design, or our scientists *could* invent—could if they had plenty of time—will neither defend us nor retaliate. Even in World War II, the mobilization of our potential strength was almost too late. Hitler's economic base was much smaller than the Allies' potential, but his headstart almost won for him twice, once in the Battle of Britain and again in his last-minute rocket offensive. In World War III, we may not have days, much less years.

Second, military strength is not achieved by making civilian goods. The way to become strong in producing aircraft is to produce aircraft and to build plants that produce aircraft. The way to have scientists and engineers skilled in missiles development is to develop missiles. Let us not fool ourselves that the use of talent and other resources to design, say, more automatic and more powerful automobiles is contributing to our national strength. Why was the United States the strongest power in the world in 1946? The plant capacity, the know-how, the technological lead that gave us our pre-eminent position (unimpaired, through our geographical good fortune, by any wartime devastation) were substantially the work of the war itself. If now the Soviet Union has overtaken us, it is not because their over-all productive capacity exceeds ours—it still falls far short. But in the grim calculus of relative military strength, much of our vast production is just thrown away, while they have concentrated on building the capacity and advancing the technology of military strength.

Third, growth of our productive power requires expansion of government activities—federal, state, and local—as well as expansion of private activities. In the ideology of the Humphreys and the Byrds, dollars spent by governments are *prima facie* unproductive, dollars spent by private individuals and firms productive. In the eighteenth century the Physiocrats regarded only the tillers of land as productive; the remainder of society, no matter how busy, were viewed as unproductive parasites. Even Adam Smith reserved the adjective "productive" for makers of tangible goods, though he was willing to count artisans as well as farmers. Fortunately neither of these views was permitted to interfere with Western economic development. The derogation of the public servant (and of those whose pay is indirectly due to government) is a more recent and unhappily more serious version of the same fallacy. Government dollars spent for such things as fire and police protection, education, postal service, highways, parks, hospitals, libraries, sanitation, and flood control, need have no inferiority complex with respect to private dollars spent for steaks, television, freezers, alcohol, horse racing, gasoline, comic books, and golf. Classical economic ideology invests the processes by which private firms and households decide how much and on what to spend with rationality, sanctity, and purity. In contrast, the decision mechanisms of politics and bureaucracy are regarded as haphazard and often sordid. This contrast can be maintained only by an unduly cynical view of democratic political processes and an excessively idealized picture of the decision processes of consumers and businessmen. Do rational choices always come from consumers beset on every side by the cleverest stratagems of Madison Avenue? Can we be so sure of the wisdom of corporation managements contending with inadequate information about the future and with the conflicting pressures of their own constituent interest groups—stockholders, employees, customers, and creditors?

Finally, what of the gloomy prophecies that high rates of taxation will destroy the vitality of American capitalism by removing the incentives for effort and for risk-taking? While their public spokesmen have bombarded us with these predictions of calamity for twenty years or more, American businessmen have striven as earnestly and diligently as ever and the corporations they manage have engineered an unparalleled expansion of capital at risk in new plant and equipment. It is time to base economic policy on the evidence of history rather than on imaginary future catastrophes.

(3) One justification of the bearish assessment of American capabilities that has dominated defense and budget policy is the fear that large budgets and high taxes would inhibit over-all economic growth. In view of the overriding importance assigned to economic growth, it is ironic that the Administration has permitted our rate of growth to be retarded in the past two years in spite of, or perhaps because of, the restriction in government activity. This retardation is because of the third besetting fear that has shaped the economic policies of the Administration, the fear of inflation.

All good people dislike inflation, just as they oppose rainy weekends and traffic accidents. But, like many other evils, inflation is not an absolute and must be viewed in the perspective of competing evils. A society can suffer much worse maladies than inflation: for example, war, illiteracy, juvenile delinquency, racial disharmony, inadequate medical care. Our postwar inflation decade has also been a decade of unparalleled prosperity and improvement in standards of living.

Why is inflation in such bad repute? Most people make no distinction between moderate and gradual inflation (say 2-4 percent per year) and certain notorious runaway inflations (100-1000 percent per year) like that in Germany after World War I or in Japan after World War II. Though it is widely pontificated that the first variety invariably leads to the second, there is no evidence to support this view; and the postwar examples of the United States, Britain, and a number of other Western countries so far refute it. A common denominator of disastrous inflations is the occurrence of severe shocks to the entire political, economic, and social fabric of the society: devastation or defeat in war, revolution, reparations, or other heavy external obligations. Under the impact of such cataclysms the population loses confidence in the currency and in other government obligations. Obviously the circumstances that gradually push up the price level in peacetime United States are of an entirely different order.

The other main reason for inflation's bad name is that lenders of all kinds—people with currency in the mattress, investors in government bonds, holders of mortgages, owners of life insurance, savings depositors, etc.—are repaid in coin of less purchasing power than they lent. Small savers in particular do not realize the risks they run in acquiring fixed-money-value assets and need to be protected from these risks. Investors with more wealth and better information are able to hedge against inflation by investing in common stocks or other claims to real property. It is a major defect of our financial structure that inflation hedges are not available for the majority of the population; American inventiveness and ingenuity have been sadly lacking in this area. The government could issue bonds with purchasing-power guarantees, and life insurance companies could offer "variable" annuities to protect beneficiaries against inflation. Some of the energy spent in denouncing inflation—and the more difficult it seems to be to control, the more loudly it is denounced—could better be spent in designing institutions that mitigate its inequities. It would not be hard to make inflation innocuous even to investors of limited means and knowledge.

The main inflationary consequences of government expenditure can and should be avoided by resolute taxation. But even if the budget is balanced, inflation may result from an excess of private demands over the resources available to satisfy them or from private pressures for increasing money incomes at rates excessive in relation to the growth of productivity.

The Federal Reserve System can fight inflation with "tight money"; and beginning in 1956, we have been sacrificing some production, and some growth in our productive capacity, to the anti-inflationary objectives of the Administration and the Federal Reserve. The evidences of the sacrifice are numerous: increasing unemployment, reduction in weekly hours of work and in overtime, withdrawal of women and young people from the labor force, retardation of the rate of growth of total output, decline of industrial production, excess capacity in steel and other industries. The Federal Reserve has deliberately kept credit tight enough to produce some slack in the economy, in the hope that the rate of price increase (running at 3 or 4 percent per year) will be moderated. So far this hope has not been justified, and indeed it is not clear that the main sources of the inflation are vulnerable to any weapons at the disposal of the Federal Reserve. No one but Mr. Martin knows how much slack the Federal Reserve is willing to force upon the economy in the effort to stop inflation. Even after the Federal Reserve gave, in November, 1957, belated recognition to the recession all other observers detected months before, its actions were mainly passive and symbolic. By the end of January, the "Fed" had yet to give the banks a significant transfusion of new reserves to enable them to increase their lending.

It is true that tight money weeds out many highly dispensable uses of resources; to a certain extent the more urgent needs are the ones that can pay the higher interest rates and qualify for credit accommodation. But the victims of tight money are also public investment programs—in education, public health, urban redevelopment—that the nation can ill afford to postpone. Some mechanism for moderating these effects of tight money is urgently needed.

The American people have entrusted military judgments to the military man they have installed in the White House. When all else fails, the defense budget is defended against critical attacks from both directions by appeal to his authority. President Eisenhower would not take chances with the nation's security. President Eisenhower would not say we needed so large a budget unless we really do. Whatever one may think of the President's ability to assess our military and diplomatic position, these appeals to his authority omit the other half of the considerations relevant to his budgetary decisions. If it is a question of cutting the defense budget, the risks to our security and to the position of the free world must be balanced against the gains to our economy and to our civilian standard of life. If it is a question of increasing the defense budget, the improvements in our military and diplomatic position must be weighed against the losses to our private economy and our consumption standards. Even if President Eisenhower is a reliable expert on the military side of this balance, no one has suggested that he is an authority on the economic side. Concerning the seriousness of changes in the budget for the short-run and long-run vigor of the economy and well-being of the population, he has relied on Secretary Humphrey. The result is that he has greatly overestimated the weight of the considerations that oppose defense spending and other governmental programs.

The President's budget for 1958-59 shows the continuing force of this tragic overestimate. Though billed in headlines as the largest peacetime budget ever, it actually represents a reduction in the physical volume of goods and services to be purchased by the government. This is true both of the budget as a whole and of its defense component. The illusion of increase is due to rises in the costs of the goods and services the government buys. The budget means a smaller flow of product to the federal government in absolute terms, and it means an even greater reduction in the government's relative share of our growing national capacity to produce. Public concern has prodded a reluctant President to propose modest increases in spending for missiles and other new weapons, foreign aid, federal scholarships, and scientific research. But in his view these increases must be met by curtailments of other federal programs, mostly other defense programs. If he must request federal money for scholarships and science, then he evidently feels he cannot ask again for funds for school construction. The President does not consider the possibility that many private uses of resources might be much more logical candidates for sacrifice than governmental programs, defense or non-defense. Indeed his budget leaves the way clear for *all* of the growing capacity of the economy to be channeled into still further elevation of our standards of luxury.

The American people, it is often said, don't want to pay the enormous costs of national security. They are not willing, it is said, to pay the taxes necessary to keep the Western World ahead in basic science, in weapons research and development, in armaments in being. They are tired, it is alleged, of the drain on their resources involved in our peaceful competition with Communism for the economic development of the new nations of Africa and Asia.

What the American people decide they want depends on how well their leaders inform them about the dangers the country and the world face. They have gladly acquiesced in the mood of complacency and indulgence fostered by the Eisenhower Administration. But their entire history leaves no doubt that they would also rise to a challenge frankly presented by a leadership genuinely alert to the dangers confronting the free world. The Russian satellites may shake the American people from their complacency and cause them to demand the kind of leadership that elected democratic leaders are supposed to provide without prompting from their followers. Sputnik will be well worth the blow it has dealt our national pride if it frees national policy from the shackles of fiscal orthodoxy. The Treasury and Defense Departments are under new leaders, like their predecessors men who have demonstrated their capabilities for practical leadership in private affairs. If they carry to their new jobs the pragmatic approach that led to their private success, our policy may yet be determined by the needs of the age rather than by ancient ideology.

NORMAN A. GRAEBNER

Eisenhower's Popular Leadership

AFTER ALMOST eight years in the White House, Dwight D. Eisenhower remains the most enigmatic phenomenon in the history of the American Presidency. Never has a popular leader who dominated so completely the national political scene affected so negligibly the essential historic processes of his time. Never has a President so renowned for his humanitarian instincts avoided so assiduously all the direct challenges to the status of individual civil rights. Promoted in 1952 as the man best qualified to deal with the Russians, he has resolved or mitigated none of the cold war conflicts which existed when he assumed office. Elected with an unshakable reputation in military affairs, he has met expanding criticism from military experts for his primary decisions on national defense. Heralded as a man of peace, he has entered his last months in office with the United States subjected to humiliating and unprecedented abuse in many areas of the free world.

This evident dichotomy between the popular image of the President and the net gains of his leadership is a simple and disturbing expression of that traditional American philosophy which denies politics a distinct and honorable place in national affairs. American society has long admired personality more than political wisdom, technique more than substance, honesty more than judgment. In a nation where private virtues have become the measure for public as well as private action, the President's transparent goodness and integrity alone have permitted him to escape direct responsibility for the nation's performance at home and abroad.

But Eisenhower as a political phenomenon has also been the product of his times, for he has fit the 1950's like a glove. Prosper-

"Eisenhower's Popular Leadership" by Norman A. Graebner is from the October 1960 issue of *Current History*. Reprinted by permission of Current History, Inc.

ity, by 1953, had eliminated most of the direct economic and social challenges of the past and with them the hard contest of power which characterizes politics in periods of stress. This absence of pervading strife has contributed to the nation's complacency and sustained the illusion that good will is sufficient for successful leadership. When the President has failed to achieve what was expected of him, the country has excused the failure as either inconsequential or the product of perversity in others.

For Republican leaders, therefore, the task of maintaining Eisenhower's popularity has consisted largely in keeping the American people mindful of his personal attributes. Republican editors, whether motivated by the President's obvious good intentions or by the knowledge that for a minority party he has been the greatest asset in over a generation, have given him the most adulatory press coverage in American history. The principle that right intent is of the essence has permitted White House officials to isolate Eisenhower from his policies. Indeed, even those Democratic leaders in Congress who have lampooned most things that the Administration has done have been careful not to blame the President directly.

That Eisenhower's personality would become the dominant fact of American politics in the 1950's was apparent even before his nomination. As a purely military figure he was clearly one of the most "available" candidates in the nation's experience. His widely publicized and genuine personal charm, added to an illustrious military reputation at a time when such a reputation had some relevance to the requirements for successful leadership, made his selection by the Republican convention synonymous with his election to the White House.

Beyond Eisenhower's personal popularity nothing in the 1952 election was clear. The Republican candidate was not offered to the nation as the exponent of any specific economic faith. His personal "creed" had been published in the New York *Herald Tribune* prior to his nomination; it avowed a fundamental economic conservatism in which he warned that too much federal intervention would turn "the American dream into an American nightmare." But such views were not publicized, and Republican campaigning avoided any open clash with established Democratic economic dogma.

In electing Eisenhower, the nation demanded nothing more than a kind of independent leadership from a great personality who could rise above the strife of party. It was this quality in him that brought millions of stay-at-homes to the polls to produce a landslide victory. Eisenhower had not shattered the Democratic party. Adlai Stevenson, his Democratic opponent, received 3,000,000 more votes than did Harry Truman in 1948.

Dominating the new Administration in January, 1953, were representatives of the managerial class—the highly-paid men hired to manage the great industrial and commercial enterprises of the country. This new class had thrown its corporate power behind Eisenhower in 1952; now it provided two-thirds of his original appointments to Cabinet and key administrative posts. This group interpreted the election as a clarion call to effect a conservative revolution.

Whatever the composition and intent of the new leadership, it could not ignore the twin legacies of the past—the New Deal and the cold war. Republican leaders might speak the rhetoric of free enterprise, but in the essential areas of national action they deviated scarcely from the Truman tradition. Secretary Humphrey could neither dismantle the budget nor halt the continuing inflation. Nor could Secretary Benson return the American farmer to free enterprise. Eventually he would hand out more in agricultural subsidies than any of his Democratic predecessors.

The "New Look" in military policy spelled out the Administration's effort to fulfill its promise of tax reduction without endangering the nation. The President made it clear that he was tailoring military power to budgetary considerations. In May, 1953, he suggested a budget cut of $8 billion to achieve "maximum military strength within economic capacities." A healthy and functioning economy, he said, was inseparable from true defense.

Eventually the New Look resulted in the burgeoning emphasis on nuclear weapons, for with such weapons the nation could achieve maximum destructiveness at minimum cost. Military experts warned that the concentration on such weapons limited the nation's strategic flexibility and, in the event of aggression, narrowed the American response to inaction or the mushroom cloud. The President held his own simply by throwing his personal prestige behind the Administration's basic military decisions.

Necessity had taken its toll of Republican ambitions. Occasional legislation like Tidelands Oil or the Dixon-Yates contract caught the old spirit, but most bills resembled the remnants of the New Deal. Never had a national leadership been forced to operate so completely outside its established philosophy. This, in essence, spelled out the Republican dilemma. With its deep allegiance to American business, the administration refused to modify or restate its neo-Hooverian beliefs. It talked the language of Main Street, but Main Street does not control elections.

What remained in the Republican arsenal were the alleged failures in Truman foreign policy that had been exploited effectively in the 1952 campaign. For the Taftites in Congress, foreign policy had become the pawn in the conservative revolution, with American failures in the Far East attributed to Democratic subversion and even New Dealism itself. Through congressional investigation the Republican leadership in Congress proceeded to delve into everything from past treason and corruption to the decisions of the Korean War.

Eisenhower did nothing to prevent this continuing Republican assault on the Democratic past although Democratic support was essential for the success of his program in Congress. His Administration quickly came to terms with Senator Joseph McCarthy of Wisconsin as the price of party unity. In exchange for Administration silence the Wisconsin Senator agreed to attack nothing that occurred after January 20, 1953. Eventually the Administration itself became implicated in offering the diet of "warmed-over spy" when Herbert Brownell, the Attorney General, resurrected the Harry Dexter White case in 1953. As the Administration, under Executive Order 10450, relieved hundreds from the federal payroll, it never made clear the nature of the charges.

Democratic leaders never forced the President to pay the political price for silencing his own right wing for their support in Congress. The foreign aid bill of 1953, for example, passed an almost equally divided House with 160 Democratic and 119 Republican votes. On critical matters of foreign affairs it was the Democratic party that carried the Administration's program. These Democratic votes, for which nothing was required, permitted Eisenhower to escape the internal warfare of his party.

Sharp Republican reverses in November, 1953, demonstrated that the party leadership had not found a satisfactory formula. Republican chairman Leonard W. Hall admitted, "There is no question about it—as of today we are in trouble politically." To liberal Republicans there was an answer. The party required essentially a restatement of its philosophy that would form a better compromise between the past and present. Jacob K. Javits of New York suggested that liberal Republicanism contained the balance that would meet the challenge of American politics. "Republican progressives," he wrote in *The New York Times Magazine* of November 15, 1953,

subscribe whole-heartedly to the principle of individual freedom and to the idea of an economic system of competitive, private enterprise functioning with government help and co-operation rather than under government domination. But they also hold that belief in free enterprise does not eliminate a wide area of activities in which government can and should provide the individual's welfare by providing him with greater opportunities for social improvement than he could otherwise obtain.

Eisenhower grasped at the new formula. The government, he explained, believed in a program that was liberal with respect to public needs but conservative in matters of finance. In his message of January, 1954, he promised the business community that it would be expected to meet the basic need of an expanding economy. But the government, he added, would face the issues of welfare, social security, health, education and housing. "Banishing of destitution and cushioning the shock of personal disaster on the individual," he said, "are proper concerns of all levels of government, including the federal government."

Republican writers such as Arthur Larson, author of *A Republican Looks at his Party,* accepted the challenge of giving the new consensus the stature of a philosophy which was neither old Republicanism or New Dealism. They insisted that Eisenhower had become the architect and embodiment of a coherent political movement which had an entity of its own and which would continue after him. In a sense the new Republicanism reflected the President's amorphous vision of the general good which could best be achieved with moderation in everything. To describe his program, the President applied the terms "moderate progressivism" and "progressive moderation."

Essentially the new middle represented Republican conservatism which had made its bargain with the New Deal. As such it was an apt expression of the times, not a new philosophy of government. It simply reflected the conviction that policies of moderation are most suitable for times of prosperity. Efficiency and decentralization are natural goals in any post-crisis period.

Eventually the new Republicanism was reduced to an effort to explain the nation's high prosperity in terms of expanded economic freedom under the new Republican hegemony. At times it even identified prosperity with American virtues—a strong devotion to the family, the urge to work and save, the ambition to excel. Nowhere did Republican faith harbor the slightest doubt that the new balance had cured the business cycle. Assuming the persistence of prosperity, it contained no body of thought to guide the nation when things went wrong. It was not concerned with innovation or foreign affairs.

Actually the nation had long been moving toward what has been called the Eisenhower equilibrium. But the movement was prompted more by the mood of complacency and the conviction that enough had been done than by the attraction of any new economic doctrine. At the heart of the new center stood the conservative Democrats who after 1954 managed the affairs of Congress. With them were the Eisenhower Republicans of 1952 strengthened by the increasing conversion of Old Guard Republicans through political, economic and diplomatic necessity. Both groups agreed that the economy was basically sound and that the United States could not escape its challenges abroad. In the new consensus was an almost unprecedented feeling of interparty comradeship which blurred party distinctions. It left little room for the extremes in national political affairs. But the new center would last only as long as the nation's prosperity. Any serious cracking of the economy would again send politicians and the public scurrying to the edges of the political spectrum in search of answers and action.

Eisenhower's concept of his office was humble, even deferential, when compared to that of successful Presidents of the past. He had little taste for politics—the struggle for power among rival interests. Claiming no constitutional prerogatives for the executive branch, he pledged himself to restore confidence between the President and Congress so that both branches might work "with patience and good will to insure that the government is not divided against itself."

Eisenhower viewed his role as that of a presiding officer who exhorted and proposed, but who refused to enforce party discipline. Congressmen, he has said repeatedly, have a right to vote their own consciences.

Eisenhower was by training and habit a man of action, not of ideas. Abstractions never meant so much to him as things. For that reason the White House organization was designed to keep intellectual conflict within the Administration to a minimum. Sherman Adams, White House Chief of Staff, controlled the information coming into the White House. James C. Hagerty, White House Press Secretary, controlled the information that came out. Together they managed to keep the President almost completely isolated. The President had never acquired the habit of reading the newspapers when he was in the Army; nor did he develop the habit after he entered the White House. He secured his news largely through the Army system of being "briefed" by spokesmen of Central Intelligence, the Pentagon, the State Department, or the White House staff.

Nor had the President any greater interest in other outside sources of information. Washington officials complained that they could not reach the President. Occasionally he conferred with Republican leaders in formal meetings, with White House aides sitting in.

Eisenhower once explained why he refused to become involved in details. "I do not believe," he informed a press conference, "that any individual . . . can do the best job just sitting at a desk and putting his face in a bunch of papers." It was his purpose, he added, "to keep his mind free of inconsequential details" so that he could make "clearer and better judgments." The President constructed his White House staff to eliminate the burden of detail.

Some writers have become ecstatic over Eisenhower's concept and use of his Cabinet. They have prophesied that this organization, with its regularly scheduled meetings and carefully prepared agenda, will remain an integral part of the American governmental system. Perhaps the uniqueness of the system, relying on papers prepared by the executive departments, rests in the fact that it is admirably designed to achieve a broad consensus on administrative decisions. Eisenhower has viewed his administrative machine as partially a military staff, partially a board of directors.

The cohesion and loyalty of the White House team was a controlling factor in the President's willingness to run for a second term. "It's taken four years to get this outfit into top working shape," he told a friend. "It would be a shame to wash it out just as they are reaching their peak efficiency." If the staff system has secured the President's objectives of consensus and efficiency, it has also led to a diffusion of responsibility, illustrated most clearly in the U-2 incident of May, 1960.

Eisenhower has refused to permit his official duties to interfere with hunting, golfing and bridge. He has sought relaxation at every opportunity away from Washington, usually at his Gettysburg farm or at the Augusta National Golf Club. Occasionally he has taken a vacation in the West or New England. He once explained to a Washington press conference that recreation was essential to maintain the fitness necessary to meet the demands of the Presidency. Hagerty has made it clear that when the President is absent from Washington a courier plane brings official papers every other day. In addition, the President often confers with officials in Washington by telephone, although more than once he has revealed extreme impatience at being disturbed by official calls from the capital.

Most Presidents have sought relief from the burdens of office. It was to the President's critics simply a matter of balance, and many believed that too often golf took precedence over matters of state. Edward P. Morgan of A.B.C. quipped characteristically in April, 1960: "President Eisenhower had hoped to helicopter to Gettysburg to cast his ballot today but found his schedule too tight. At the last minute, however, he did manage to squeeze in a round of golf."

Undoubtedly Eisenhower's concern for things material has had its effect on the intellectual climate of Washington. Many of the experts who drifted into Washington as economic and foreign policy advisers soon left. In every area of public policy the most impressive writers and thinkers are not only outside the government service but also almost totally ignored by those who make policy. Noting the absence of intellect in the nation's capital, James Reston of *The New York Times* Washington staff, complained in December, 1957:

> We are in a race with the pace of history. We are in a time when brain power is more important than fire power, but in the last five years, the President has gradually drifted apart from the intellectual opinion of the country, filled up his social hours with bantering locker-room cronies, and denied himself the mental stimulus that is always available to any President.

Whatever the nature of Eisenhower's leadership, his personality remained the unquestioned phenomenon in Presidential politics. His image was that of a well-meaning man standing at the center of American life. Never was its impact clearer than at the San Francisco convention of 1956. Eisenhower was the convention; he was the party. He was beyond challenge. Much of the President's power, ironically, resulted from his party's decline during his first term.

This commanding position was also the product of the President's new look. Under Hagerty's coaching Eisenhower had learned to dominate the Washington press conference—an exceedingly important method of shaping the public impression of the President. By 1954, he was completely at ease, often bantering with reporters. He was increasingly better informed. He had learned to dodge questions for which he had no ready answer, avoiding the "bloopers" of his early months. Republican professionals now called him the greatest instinctive politician since F.D.R.

Eisenhower's television style, assiduously cultivated by professionals, had become technically perfect. Television, in fact, provided party managers with the perfect medium for maintaining the Eisenhower image, for what mattered was not the intellectual content of his speeches, but the sincerity and warmth which he communicated to the public.

The Eisenhower personality overshadowed the Presidency itself. The traditional duties and obligations of office appeared inconsequential when contrasted with the warm and easy smile, the beaming face, the informal, simple and unpretentious manner that captured the imagination of people everywhere. Even the most popular Presidents of the past had begun to lose much of their lustre long before they left the White House. But Eisenhower's stature continued to grow.

With the new look the President revealed more determination in office, more familiarity with issues. He spoke less of co-operation with Congress and more about defending the prerogatives of the executive. But energy and action are not the sole criteria for effective leadership. With his increased interest in the exercise of his powers the President demonstrated no new awareness of the great political forces in the world, no new evidence that he had any greater interest in ideas. Often he seemed to be placing his new leadership in the service of drift, providing, in the words of Richard H. Rovere, "the spectacle, novel in the history of the Presidency, of a man strenuously in motion yet doing essentially nothing—traveling all the time yet going nowhere."

The difficulty was not the President's firmness; it was the nature of his policies. It was less the decisiveness than the decisions themselves. Despite the energy behind them, Eisenhower's actions still suggested that there were no problems that good intentions would not cure.

Sustaining the Eisenhower image did little for the Republican organization. Party managers sought to exploit the President's personality. They succeeded merely in assuring the American people that whatever happened, the President, not the party, would assume the burdens of leadership. This accounts for the strange dichotomy between the President's growing popularity and the persistent decline in Republican strength. Republican Governor Theodore R.

McKeldin of Maryland reminded a Republican audience in February, 1957, that the party "hasn't a thing that the country wants" except Eisenhower. Nowhere had the Republican party succeeded in turning the President's image into any genuine political gains.

What has characterized the Eisenhower foreign policies has been the substitution of principle and personality for the traditional ingredients of diplomacy. In large measure this approach was dictated by the successful Republican campaigning of 1952. For when the Republican leadership, with its rhetoric of liberation, promised no less than the dismantling of both the Iron and Bamboo curtains, it denied itself the freedom to create future policy compatible with limited American power. Only when that leadership had disposed of its political symbols of Democratic iniquity and admitted publicly that it could not achieve what its key spokesmen, including the President, continued to promise during the months of party consolidation, could it formulate policy goals that had some relationship to the means at its disposal.

So completely had party objectives abroad over-reached American interest that the President's noteworthy achievements lay in *not* doing what members of his party demanded. His stature in the area of foreign affairs rested in his *refusal* to engage in war against mainland China, to become involved in the Indo-Chinese civil war, to employ massive retaliation against Chinese cities.

It was the contribution of Secretary of State John Foster Dulles to translate American demands on Moscow and Peking, anchored to domestic political requirements, to the high realm of principle. If politics and principle converged, it was because both sought the retreat of the Soviet bloc. To that extent Dulles' principles appeared to square with American security interests, and the fact that through six years they exceeded what this nation's power could achieve and prevented the settlement of every outstanding issue in the cold war seemed to make no difference. If United States leadership could not secure what it wanted of others, it could at least take comfort in its ideals.

Unfortunately this reduced Mr. Dulles' diplomacy to rhetoric, for nothing else remained. As Hans J. Morgenthau wrote in December, 1956:

> When we heard spokesmen for the government propound the legal and moral platitudes which had passed for foreign policy in the interwar period, we thought that this was the way in which the government—as all governments must—tried to make the stark facts of for-

eign policy palatable to the people. . . . We were mistaken. Those platitudes *are* the foreign policy of the United States. . . .

If Dulles settled nothing, he also gave nothing away. The result of his tenure as Secretary of State was stalemate—a stalemate in which the cold war shifted to intense military and economic competition. Here Dulles' leadership could not prevent sharp reverses in Western power and prestige.

With Dulles' death in 1959 American policy became equated with the personality of the President. The rhetoric of liberation, now anchored to such homilies as "peace under freedom" or "peace with justice," continued, but even more important in the new diplomacy was the very person of the President. State visits abroad would give him the opportunity to demonstrate his good will before the world. Thereafter his success was measured not by diplomatic settlement but by the size and enthusiasm of the crowds that lined the thoroughfares of the cities of Europe, Asia and Latin America when he visited. These pressing throngs gave the impression that this nation was at last winning the cold war.

Unfortunately there was always the marked dichotomy between the cheers of the crowds and the lack of diplomatic progress in the chancelleries. Eisenhower's world travels were continuing expressions of American good intent, but they encompassed no action, commitments, or positive ideas to give permanent meaning to the tours. What remained after the experience was the evidence of personality and the absence of concrete achievement.

It was ironic that the President's good will tour of the Orient should be marred by Tokyo mobs, for the new diplomacy had been directed toward mobs. The President had been warned by writers, editors and even members of Congress, after the collapse of the Paris summit conference of May, 1960, not to run the risk of a trip around the fringes of the Communist world in the Far East. But to men who equated large crowds with diplomatic success here was the easiest method available to prove that the United States had lost nothing at Paris. What the cheers at Taipei and Tokyo might achieve was not clear. Had the President managed his trip to Japan he would have measured the triumph by the shouts of the people, for there was little to be gained in the quiet of the Japanese Foreign Office.

In a sense, Eisenhower's world tours comprised a final effort to create the illusion of peace when all genuine diplomacy had ceased to exist. What seemed to matter was the President's ability to draw larger and more enthusiastic crowds than Premier Khrushchev.

But the visit of a president or premier to another land has no function other than to expose the visiting dignitary to the people that jam the thoroughfares. It is a mutual demonstration of good will, but nothing more. For if actual diplomacy were the objective, that could be pursued more cheaply and effectively via normal diplomatic channels. Nothing better illustrates the ephemeral nature of state visits than Khrushchev's conviction that he had won over the support of the American public during his remarkable visit of September, 1959. In retrospect, the visit had no effect on Russian-American relations at all.

Eisenhower responded to his failures in Paris and Tokyo with an air of injured innocence. His own dignity amid the collapse of the summit created the impression that whatever went wrong he was not at fault. He continued to detach himself from personal responsibility or the opinion of the free world. For the loss of American prestige in the Far East he blamed the Communists, not the deep and reasonable doubts created by missiles and Soviet threats. He continued to identify world peace with his personal diplomacy, repeating this conviction after his return from the Orient in July, 1960:

> No consideration of personal fatigue or inconvenience, no threat or argument would deter me from once again setting out on a course that has meant much for our country, for her friends, and for the cause of freedom—and peace with justice in the world.

Always the sacrifice was to the person, not to the nation in the form of added strength or reduced ambitions. In equating the cause of peace with the enthusiasm he received abroad, the President forgot that it is this nation's relations with the governments at Moscow and Peking, not with the crowds of New Delhi, Paris, or Taipei, that matter. In denying any error in judgment or policy, the President permitted no official review of his record. This solved no problems, but merely swept them under the rug.

Eisenhower's leadership has given rise to a curious standard of appraisal. For almost eight years his adherents have measured his success by popularity, not achievement. As George E. Allen concluded in his *Saturday Evening Post* article on Eisenhower in April, 1960:

> The man who took office mistrusting politics and politicians will leave office having proved himself one of the most successful politicians ever to occupy the Presidency. He will leave the White House more popular than when he moved in, and this will be an unprecedented feat—a political feat.

By such standards of personal popularity Harding and Coolidge would rank among the most successful of American presidents; Washington, John Adams, Polk, Lincoln, and Wilson among the failures.

What matters far more in Presidential success are, first, the intellectual alertness necessary to penetrate contemporary movements and, second, the political craftsmanship required to translate victory into political action which meets the challenge of the times. Measured by its adaptation of the Democratic past to the conditions of the 1950's, the Eisenhower leadership had been a success, indeed an historical necessity. But the permanent judgment of that leadership will hinge on the President's achievement in influencing, within the limits of his power, the fundamental trends of this age toward the protection of this nation's well-being.

The recent past is interlude. The dilemmas of the 1950's await their disposal in some future time. Only in that future will men be permitted to judge finally whether the present leadership has prepared the nation mentally and physically for the cataclysm that is sure to come.

DWIGHT D. EISENHOWER

Farewell Address

GOOD EVENING, MY FELLOW AMERICANS:

First, let me express my gratitude to the radio and television networks for the opportunity to express myself to you during these past eight years and tonight.

Three days from now, after half a century in the service of our country, I shall lay down the responsibilities of office as, in traditional solemn ceremony, the authority of the President is vested in my successor.

This evening I come to you with a message of leave-taking and farewell, and to share a few final thoughts with you, my countrymen.

Like every other citizen, I wish the new President, and all who will labor with him, Godspeed. I pray that the coming years will be blessed with peace and prosperity for all. Our people expect their President and the Congress to find essential agreement on issues of great moment, the wise resolution of which will better shape the future of the nation.

My own relations with the Congress, which began on a remote and tenuous basis when, long ago, a member of the Senate appointed me to West Point, have since ranged to the intimate during the war and the immediate post-war period, and, finally to the mutually interdependent during these past eight years.

In this final relationship, the Congress and the Administration have, on most vital issues, co-operated well, to serve the national good rather than mere partisanship, and so have assured the business of the nation should go forward. So, my official relationship with the Congress ends in a feeling, on my part, of gratitude that we have been able to do so much together.

We now stand ten years past the midpoint of a century that has witnessed four major wars among great nations. Three of these in-

Delivered in Washington, January 18, 1961.

volved our own country. Despite these holocausts America is today the strongest, the most influential, and most productive nation in the world. Understandably proud of this pre-eminence, we yet realize that America's leadership and prestige depend, not merely upon our unmatched material progress, riches, and material strength, but on how we use our power in the interests of world peace and human betterment.

Throughout America's adventure in free government, our basic purposes have been to keep the peace; to foster progress in human achievement; and to enhance liberty, dignity, and integrity among people and among nations. To strive for less would be unworthy of a free and religious people. Any failure traceable to arrogance, or our lack of comprehension or readiness to sacrifice would inflict upon us grievous hurt both at home and abroad.

Progress toward these noble goals is persistently threatened by the conflict now engulfing the world. It commands our whole attention, absorbs our very beings. We face a hostile ideology—global in scope, atheistic in character, ruthless in purpose, and insidious in method. Unhappily the danger it poses promises to be of indefinite duration. To meet it successfully, there is called for, not so much the emotional and transitory sacrifices of crisis, but rather those which enable us to carry forward steadily, surely, and without complaint the burdens of a prolonged and complex struggle—with liberty the stake. Only thus shall we remain, despite every provocation, on our chartered course toward permanent peace and human betterment.

Crises there will continue to be. In meeting them, whether foreign or domestic, great or small, there is a recurring temptation to feel that some spectacular and costly action could become the miraculous solution to all current difficulties. A huge increase in newer elements of our defense; development of unrealistic programs to cure every ill in agriculture; a dramatic expansion in basic and applied research—these and many other possibilities, each possibly promising in itself, may be suggested as the only way to the road we wish to travel.

But each proposal must be weighed in the light of a broader consideration: the need to maintain balance in and among national problems—balance between the private and the public economy, balance between cost and hoped for advantage—balance between the clearly necessary and the comfortably desirable; balance between our essential requirements as a nation and the duties imposed by the nation upon the individual; balance between actions of the moment and the national welfare of the future. Good judgment seeks balance and progress; lack of it eventually finds imbalance and frustration.

The record of many decades stands as proof that our people and their government have, in the main, understood these truths and have responded to them well, in the face of stress and threat. But threats, new in kind or degree, constantly arise. I mention two only.

A vital element in keeping the peace is our military establishment. Our arms must be mighty, ready for instant action, so that no potential aggressor may be tempted to risk his own destruction.

Our military organization today bears little relation to that known by any of my predecessors in peacetime, or indeed by the fighting men in World War II or Korea.

Until the latest of our world conflicts, the United States had no armaments industry. American makers of plowshares could, with time and as required, make swords as well. But now we can no longer risk emergency improvision of national defense; we have been compelled to create a permanent armaments industry of vast proportions. Added to this, three and a half million men and women are directly engaged in the defense establishment. We annually spend on military security more than the net income of all United States corporations.

This conjunction of an immense military establishment and a large arms industry is new in American experience. The total influence—economic, political, even spiritual—is felt in every city, every state house, every office of the federal government. We recognize the imperative need for this development. Yet we must not fail to comprehend its grave implications. Our toil, resources and livelihood are all involved; so is the very structure of our society.

In the councils of government, we must guard against the acquisition of unwarranted influence, whether sought or unsought, by the military-industrial complex. The potential for the disastrous rise of misplaced power exists and will persist.

We must never let the weight of this combination endanger our liberties or democratic processes. We should take nothing for granted. Only an alert and knowledgeable citizenry can compel the proper meshing of the huge industrial and military machinery of defense with our peaceful methods and goals, so that security and liberty may prosper together.

Akin to, and largely responsible for the sweeping changes in our industrial-military posture, has been the technological revolution during recent decades.

In this revolution, research has become central; it also becomes more formalized, complex, and costly. A steadily increasing share is conducted for, by, or at the direction of, the federal government.

Today, the solitary inventor, tinkering in his shop, has been overshadowed by task forces of scientists in laboratories and testing fields. In the same fashion, the free university, historically the fountainhead of free ideas and scientific discovery, has experienced a revolution in the conduct of research. Partly because of the huge costs involved, a government contract becomes virtually a substitute for intellectual curiosity. For every old blackboard there are now hundreds of new electronic computers.

The prospect of domination of the nation's scholars by federal employment, project allocations, and the power of money is ever present and is gravely to be regarded.

Yet, in holding scientific research and discovery in respect, as we should, we must also be alert to the equal and opposite danger that public policy could itself become the captive of a scientific-technological elite.

It is the task of statesmanship to mold, to balance, and to integrate these and other forces, new and old, within the principles of our democratic system—ever aiming toward the supreme goals of our free society.

Another factor in maintaining balance involves the element of time. As we peer into society's future, we—you and I, and our government—must avoid the impulse to live only for today, plundering, for our own ease and convenience, the precious resources of tomorrow. We cannot mortgage the material assets of our grandchildren without risking the loss also of their political and spiritual heritage. We want democracy to survive for all generations to come, not to become the insolvent phantom of tomorrow.

Down the long lane of the history yet to be written America knows that this world of ours, ever growing smaller, must avoid becoming a community of dreadful fear and hate, and be, instead, a proud confederation of mutual trust and respect.

Such a confederation must be one of equals. The weakest must come to the conference table with the same confidence as do we, protected as we are by our moral, economic, and military strength. That table, though scarred by many past frustrations, cannot be abandoned for the certain agony of the battlefield.

Disarmament, with mutual honor and confidence, is a continuing imperative. Together we must learn how to compose differences, not with arms, but with intellect and decent purpose. Because this need is so sharp and apparent I confess that I lay down my official responsibilities in this field with a definite sense of disappointment. As one who has witnessed the horror and the lingering sadness of war—as one who knows that another war could utterly destroy this civilization which has been so slowly and painfully built over thousands of years—I wish I could say tonight that a lasting peace is in sight.

Happily, I can say that war has been avoided. Steady progress toward our ultimate goal has been made. But, so much remains to be done. As a private citizen, I shall never cease to do what little I can to help the world advance along that road.

So—in this my last good night to you as your President—I thank you for the many opportunities you have given me for public service in war and peace. I trust that in that service you find some things worthy; as for the rest of it, I know you will find ways to improve performance in the future.

You and I—my fellow citizens—need to be strong in our faith that all nations, under God, will reach the goal of peace with justice. May we be ever unswerving in devotion to principle, confident but humble with power, diligent in pursuit of the nation's great goals.

To all the peoples of the world, I once more give expression to America's prayerful and continuing aspiration:

We pray that peoples of all faiths, all races, all nations may have their great human needs satisfied; that those now denied opportunity shall come to enjoy it to the full; that all who yearn for freedom may experience its spiritual blessings; that those who have freedom will understand, also, its heavy responsibilities; that all who are insensitive to the needs of others will learn charity; that the scourges of poverty, disease, and ignorance will be made to disappear from the earth, and that, in the goodness of time, all peoples will come to live together in a peace guaranteed by the binding force of mutual respect and love.

Now on Friday noon I am to become a private citizen. I am proud to do so. I look forward to it.

CONTRIBUTORS

This collection of essays on the Presidency of Dwight D. Eisenhower has been compiled both for those who liked Ike, as well as for those who did not. Every effort has been made, of course, to include writings, neither partisan nor adulatory, which present interestingly and fairly most of the major issues confronting the Eisenhower Administrations. The writers represented are all eminent in their fields. Some are university professors, others are editorialists and journalists; one is a former Assistant to the President. Taken as a whole, this collection of articles is intended to give the reader a sampling of contemporary analysis and some of the raw historical data upon which the reader may make his own estimate of President Eisenhower and Republican response to the fifties.

Sherman Adams, Congressman from New Hampshire and one-time Governor of that state, was an Assistant to the President from 1953 to 1958. The selection from his book, *Firsthand Report,* describes the operation of the White House staff under Eisenhower.

Samuel Lubell has worked as a newspaper reporter and magazine writer since the 1930's and he has appeared as an analyst and commentator on a variety of radio and television programs. His recent books, *Revolution in World Trade, The Future of American Politics,* and *Revolt of the Moderates* have been widely acclaimed. The selection from the latter volume contained here analyzes Eisenhower as a politician during the opening years of the crusade.

Professor Eric F. Goldman's *Rendezvous With Destiny* was the 1952 Bancroft Prize winner. He has taught American history at Princeton University for nearly two decades. The reprinted portion of his book, *The Crucial Decade—and After,* describes the Eisenhower Cabinet, the end of the Korean war, and the President's difficulties with Senator Joseph McCarthy.

Charles J. V. Murphy, a member of the Board of Editors of *Fortune* magazine, has for well over a decade covered news from the White House. "The Eisenhower Shift," one of a series of articles written by Murphy for *Fortune* on Republican economic and administrative policy, tells of the President's attempts to alter the welfare state economy.

Richard H. Rovere has attracted world-wide attention with his deceptively gentle "newsletters" in the *New Yorker Magazine. Affairs of State: The Eisenhower Years* is a collection of such articles written in his unique style, and is the source of Rovere's contribution here on Eisenhower's Far Eastern diplomacy.

Michael Straight has been a contributing editor to the *New Republic* since 1947. His generally approving comment on Ike's dealings with the Russians at Geneva in 1955 should be measured against such general works as Hans J. Morgenthau's articles, also written for the *New Republic,* and with W. W. Rostow's, *The United States in the World Arena.*

John Lear, since 1956 science editor for the *Saturday Review,* presents a laudatory view of one of Eisenhower's greatest proposals, the "Atoms For Peace" program. This article was originally printed in *The Reporter,* a publication not noted for its approval of Republicanism in any form.

One of the finest books yet written on the Eisenhower years is Robert J. Donovan's *Eisenhower: The Inside Story,* from which is drawn a detailed description of the President's critical illness, the management of government during his absence from Washington, and an analysis of his decision to run for a second term. Donovan, a newspaper reporter since the early New Deal period, has also written a book on former Speaker Joseph W. Martin, Jr.

James Tobin, Sterling Professor of Economics at Yale University and member of the Council of Economic Advisors, has contributed a provocative inquiry into the relationship between national security and Eisenhower's economic policy, one of the primary concerns of the second Republican Administration.

From the pen of Professor Norman A. Graebner of the University of Illinois comes the summary essay on the Eisenhower government. Professor Graebner, a specialist on American foreign policy and author of several works in the field, is also recognized as a perceptive commentator on domestic political issues.

No collection of writings on the decade of the fifties would be complete without President Eisenhower's Farewell Address, in which he warns the nation of the perils of an arms race to the American economy, and which he concludes with the prayer: " . . . that peoples of all faiths, all races, all nations, may have their great human needs satisfied; that those now denied opportunity shall come to enjoy it to the full; that all who yearn for freedom may experience its spiritual blessings; that those who have freedom will understand, also, its heavy responsibilities. . . ."

BIBLIOGRAPHY

Acheson, Dean, "Foreign Policy and Presidential Moralism," *The Reporter,* Vol. 16, No. 9 (May 2, 1957), pp. 10-14.

Adams, Sherman, *Firsthand Report*. New York, Harper & Bros., 1961.

Adler, Selig, *The Isolationist Impulse: Its Twentieth Century Reaction*. New York, Collier Books, 1961.

Agar, Herbert, *The Price of Power: America Since 1945*. Chicago, University of Chicago Press, 1957.

Alsop, Stewart, *Nixon and Rockefeller*. New York, Doubleday & Co., 1960.

Beal, John Robinson, *John Foster Dulles: A Biography*. New York, Harper & Bros., 1957.

Bell, Jack, *The Splendid Misery: The Story of the Presidency and Power Politics at Close Range*. New York, Doubleday & Co., 1960.

Benson, Ezra Taft, *Cross Fire: The Eight Years with Eisenhower*. New York, Doubleday & Co., 1962.

Brown, John Mason, *Through These Men: Some Aspects of Our Passing History*. New York, Harper & Bros., 1952-1956.

Buckley, William F., Jr., "The Tranquil World of Dwight D. Eisenhower," *The National Review,* Vol. 5, No. 3 (January 18, 1958), pp. 57-59.

Childs, Marquis W., *Eisenhower: Captive Hero*. New York, Harcourt, Brace & Co., 1958.

Cook, Fred J., *The Warfare State*. New York, Macmillan Co., 1962.

Davenport, John, "Arms and the Welfare State," *Yale Review,* Vol. XLVII, No. 3 (March 1958), pp. 333-346.

Davis, Kenneth S., *A Prophet in His Own Country: The Triumphs and Defeats of Adlai E. Stevenson*. New York, Doubleday & Co., 1957.

Divine, Robert A., *American Foreign Policy*. New York, Meridian Books, 1960.

Donovan, Robert J., *Eisenhower: The Inside Story*. New York, Harper & Bros., 1956.

Eisenhower, Dwight D., *Peace With Justice: Selected Addresses of Dwight David Eisenhower.* New York, Popular Library, 1961.

Eisenhower, Edgar, and John McCallum, *Six Roads from Abilene.* Seattle, Wood & Reber, 1960.

Goldman, Eric F., *The Crucial Decade—and After: America 1945-1960.* New York, Knopf Vintage Books, 1961.

——— "Good-By to the 'Fifties—and Good Riddance," *Harper's Magazine,* Vol. 220, No. 1316 (January 1960), pp. 27-29.

Goold-Adams, Richard, *John Foster Dulles: A Reappraisal.* New York, Appleton-Century-Crofts, 1962.

Graebner, Norman A., *Cold War Diplomacy 1945-1960.* Princeton, N.J., Van Nostrand Anvil Books, 1962.

——— "Eisenhower's Popular Leadership," *Current History,* Vol. 39, No. 230 (October 1960), pp. 230-236, 244.

Handlin, Oscar, "Do the Voters Want Moderation? The Politics of Evasion," *Commentary,* Vol. 22, No. 3 (September 1956), pp. 193-198.

Harris, Seymour E., *The Economics of the Political Parties.* New York, Macmillan Co., 1962.

Hauge, Gabriel, "Economics of Eisenhower Dynamic Conservatism," *The Commercial and Financial Chronicle,* Vol. 182, No. 5476 (October 27, 1955), pp. 1, 28-29.

Heller, Deane and David, *John Foster Dulles, Soldier for Peace.* New York, Holt, Rinehart and Winston, 1960.

Hyman, Sidney, "The Failure of the Eisenhower Presidency," *The Progressive,* Vol. 24, No. 5 (May 1960), pp. 10-13.

Johnson, Walter, *1600 Pennsylvania Avenue.* Boston, Little, Brown and Co., 1960.

Kornitzer, Bela, *The Real Nixon.* New York, Rand McNally & Co., 1960.

Lear, John, "Ike and the Peaceful Atom," *The Reporter,* Vol. 14, No. 1 (January 12, 1956), pp. 11-21.

Lubell, Samuel, *Revolt of the Moderates.* New York, Harper & Bros., 1956.

Lukacs, John, *A History of the Cold War.* New York, Doubleday & Co., 1961.

May, Ernest R., *The Ultimate Decision: The President as Commander in Chief.* New York, George Braziller, 1960.

Mazo, Earl, *Richard Nixon: A Political and Personal Portrait.* New York, Harper & Bros., 1959.

Morgenthau, Hans J., "The Decline and Fall of American Foreign Policy," *New Republic,* Vol. 135, No. 24 (December 10, 1956), pp. 11-16.

——— "What the President and Mr. Dulles Don't Know," *New Republic,* Vol. 135, No. 25 (December 17, 1956), pp. 14-18.

Murphy, Charles J. V., "The Budget and Eisenhower," *Fortune* (July 1957), pp. 96ff.

——— "The Eisenhower Shift," *Fortune* (January 1956), pp. 83ff; (February 1956), pp. 110ff; (March 1956), pp. 110ff.

——— "Eisenhower's White House," *Fortune* (July 1953), pp. 75ff.

——— "The White House Since Sputnik," *Fortune* (January 1958), pp. 98ff.

Niebuhr, Reinhold, "The Eisenhower Era," *The New Leader,* Vol. XLIII, No. 38 (October 3, 1960), pp. 3-4.

Nixon, Richard M., *Six Crises*. New York, Doubleday & Co., 1962.

Pusey, Merlo J., *Eisenhower the President*. New York, Macmillan Co., 1956.

Rostow, W. W., *The United States in the World Arena*. New York, Harper & Bros., 1960.

Rovere, Richard H., *Affairs of State: The Eisenhower Years*. New York, Farrar, Straus and Cudahy, 1956.

——— *Senator Joe McCarthy*. New York, Harcourt, Brace & Co., 1959.

——— "Eisenhower Over the Shoulder," *American Scholar,* Vol. 31, No. 2 (Spring 1962), pp. 176-179.

Seide, Ray, "How I Selected Westerns, Bought Socks & Prepared Paintings for President Eisenhower," *Esquire,* Vol. LVII, No. 3 (March 1962), pp. 47-49.

Sevareid, Eric, *Small Sounds in the Night*. New York, Alfred A. Knopf, 1956.

Shannon, William V., "Eisenhower as President: A Critical Appraisal of the Record," *Commentary,* Vol. 26, No. 5 (November 1958), pp. 390-398.

Smith, A. Merriman, *Meet Mr. Eisenhower*. New York, Harper & Bros., 1955.

——— *President's Odyssey*. New York, Harper & Bros., 1961.

Straight, Michael, "How Ike Reached the Russians at Geneva," *New Republic,* Vol. 133, No. 5 (August 1, 1955), pp. 7-11.

Tobin, James, "The Eisenhower Economy and National Security: Defense, Dollars, and Doctrines," *Yale Review,* Vol. XLVII, No. 3 (March 1958), pp. 321-334.

Tully, Andrew, "Ike's Bunkered Haven," *Collier's,* Vol. 136 (August 5, 1955), pp. 54-55.

White, William Smith, *The Taft Story*. New York, Harper & Bros., 1954.